Also by Joe Eck and Wayne Winterrowd

A Year at North Hill:
Four Seasons in a Vermont Garden

Also by Joe Eck

Elements of Garden Design

Also by Wayne Winterrowd

Annuals for Connoisseurs

Living Seasonally

THE KITCHEN GARDEN

AND THE TABLE

AT NORTH HILL

Living Seasonally

JOE ECK AND WAYNE WINTERROWD

Henry Holt and Company

New York

Henry Holt and Company, Inc.
Publishers since 1866
115 West 18th Street
New York, New York 10011

Henry Holt® is a registered trademark of
Henry Holt and Company, Inc.

Published in Canada by Fitzhenry & Whiteside Ltd.,
195 Allstate Parkway, Markham, Ontario L3R 4T8.

Library of Congress Cataloging-in-Publication Data
Eck, Joe.
Living seasonally: the kitchen garden and the table at
North Hill / Joe Eck and Wayne Winterrowd.—1st ed.
p.   cm.
Includes index.
ISBN 0-8050-4786-7 (cloth: alk. paper)
1. Vegetable gardening—Vermont.   2. Gardening—
Vermont.   3. Country life—Vermont.   4. Eck, Joe—
Homes and haunts—Vermont.   5. Winterrowd,
Wayne—Homes and haunts—Vermont.   6. Seasons—
Vermont.   I. Winterrowd, Wayne.   II. Title.
SB321.5.V5E36   1999   98-35334
635′.09743—dc21   CIP

Henry Holt books are available for special promotions
and premiums. For details contact: Director, Special Markets.

First Edition 1999
DESIGNED BY BETTY LEW

Printed in Hong Kong
All first editions are printed on acid-free paper. ∞

1   3   5   7   9   10   8   6   4   2

For
Mr. and Mrs. Walter J. Eck

ACKNOWLEDGMENTS

Whom must we thank for the writing of this book? Well, certainly first each other. For having begun by making a life together, and then a garden out of it, we wrote one book, and now we have written another. Though this second one is not precisely a sequel to *The Year at North Hill,* clearly it has sprung from the same ground, the same shared passions, the same attitude about life, about our life, here in this place. People who were interested in the first book seemed to find it important to isolate our two separate voices, to point to this or that passage as clearly belonging to one or the other of us. We ourselves could perform no such anatomy on our text. For we, at least, are assured that every sentence, every perception, came from the both of us, and that the voice of the book is hardly separable into two parts, any more than is the garden we have made together.

That debt acknowledged, there are certain other people we must thank who, though perhaps not operating at the center of things, have certainly tidied up the edges. First is AnnMarie Gorham, our colleague for four years, who makes everything so much simpler than it might otherwise be. We must also thank Helen Pratt, who has never failed us, nor shown the least anxiety about our work, even when she spent anxious hours wondering whether our text would come in on time and not be egregiously beyond our assigned word length. Ray Roberts and his staff at Henry Holt must also receive special thanks, not just for patience (which has been enormous, and always a balm) but for the solid editorial skills that have pulled our text between covers, so that it is offered in presentable form to readers.

Our debt to *Horticulture* magazine is beyond repaying with words. Especially, however, we must still thank Tom Cooper, its editor, who has been unfailing in his encouragement of the development of our garden and our writings about it. As with our previous book, some sections of this one first appeared in his magazine. We are grateful for permission to reprint them here, and more grateful still for his fine editorial pencil, which improved those sections and—we are sure of it—all our other horticultural writings over the years.

Finally, we must thank those readers of *The Year at North Hill* who were kind enough to write us, or to speak to us at horticultural conferences, to say that they had enjoyed what we had written and sometimes to offer corrections or additional information from their own experience. Even when there are two people at the work, writing, like gardening, can still sometimes be a lonely business. So we are especially grateful to those gardeners who have assured us that we are not alone, and that this peculiar thing we are up to (on most days) can, after all, be shared.

Joe Eck
Wayne Winterrowd
North Hill

Living Seasonally

Harvest

Among the many things that have bound us together now for so many years is something we discovered once, in accidental conversation: that we both constructed litanies as children, and still, as a way of seeking comfort in the face of the almost unendurable passage of time. The trick with such things was to include wonderful events that had happened and were certain to happen again—perhaps with variations, joys unexpected and unguessed at—but with a sure reliability, made so because the world, so hostile and mysterious, could not fail (*could not fail*) to acknowledge our small existences with pleasure, at least on certain days. Christmas, birthdays, Easter—all had promise and power not just because they carried the assurance of escape from a sequence of slaty, gray days, but because they would also surely come again, though one must wait for a whole year. We were both lonely children, and on some level we knew the facts that increasing maturity would make all too clear. Even as very small children we knew ourselves to be different; and so different structures, different ways of approaching reality, became necessary simply for survival.

We are sure that gardening, so often assumed to be merely a pastime or a healthy exercise (and one that increases property values, to boot) has been for others, as for us, a refuge, a space of safety, a way of gentling the hostility of the external world. The late J. C. Raulston, a great plantsman whose untimely death occurred in December of 1996, said once that he turned to plants because, as a child, he knew that they were the only things that would not hurt him. It has been reported, too, that the Empress Josephine, incarcerated in the dreadful prison at Carmes long before she married Napoleon, took pleasure in encouraging the small weeds and lichens and mosses that first came of themselves on the damp stones of her barred window. Destiny, of course, had finer plants in store for her—the roses of Malmaison, the rarest hothouse orchids, the first dahlias and geraniums cultivated in the Old World. Whether they would have mattered more to her than the lowly weeds at Carmes is a question not too hard to answer. For certain people, as for her, gardening of any sort—of whatever sort—becomes ballast against the tumult of days and the wastes of time. It is a knot that ties up all the various strands of existence, past, present, future; memory and desire; things experienced and things yet to come. For those who choose to do it and are made that way, it can become— early or late—one more justification for the accident of existence.

Within the large context of gardening, the raising of vegetables is peculiar, for the nourishment it offers is both physical and spiritual, a rare meeting of body and soul. In its pursuit, one becomes most directly a second Nature, seeding and tending and harvesting, usually in one season. There is a directness, too, a straightforwardness of process, a neatness expressed even in the rows, that makes vegetable gardening, among all other sorts one might think to practice, peculiarly satisfying. And, though all gardening creates litanies—the blooming of the first snowdrops, crocus and daffodils, roses and Joe Pye weed, the turning of autumn leaves and the appearance of the first colchicum—the maturation times of vegetables become unusually precious beads on a long string.

So, and first in spring: Egyptian onions and Lancer parsnips. Radishes, Mirabelle and Sora and Pink Beauty, Easter Egg. Jersey Giant asparagus and Purple Spear from Gurney's. Later, where spring and summer meet, lettuces—Black Seeded Simpson, Merveille de Quatres Saisons, Bibb, Oak Leaf, Red Sails, and Pirat. Mesclun, seeded in patches and looking like anonymous weeds: Misticanza, Niçoise, and Provencale. Arugula, mizuna, cress, and mache, mixed all within and also seeded separately. Spinach— Space and Tyee and Melody. Turnips, Early Market and White Milan. Chioggia beets, banded pink and orange when cross-cut, and Bull's Blood, a gift of Joy Larckcom, red in leaf, stem, and root. Bitter rapini, Montano cauliflower. Peas in glory: Thomas Laxton, Knight, Green Arrow, Tall Telephone, tiny Précoville. Pearl onions. The first broccoli in Superblend.

At midsummer: Beans, first bush: Triomphe de Farcy, Finard, Golden Roma, Royal Burgundy; then vines: Kwintus, Trionfo Violetto, Green Annelino and Yellow Annelino, Kentucky Wonder. Favas, a precious few. Early potatoes, robbed from beneath still fruitful vines: Russian Banana, Yukon Gold, Yellow Finn and Rose Finn, Caribe, Cowhorn, Ruby Crescent, and Urgenta. Seedling

Rainbow chard, always the least vivid, leaving the brightest colored stems for later show. Eggplant, Agora and Rosa Bianca and White Egg. Finocchio, fine eaten raw, sliced. Summer squash, Cocozelle and Yellow Crookneck, dread zucchini. Tiny cipollini onions, to boil whole.

By the First Birthday (Joe's): Tomatoes, now so many: Brandywine, Persimmon, Red Peach and Yellow Peach and Yellow Pear, Yellow Currant, Green Zebra, Great White, Paul Robeson and Black Banana (both black), Pruden's Purple, Striped German, and Matt's Wild Cherry. Peppers for all uses: Ancho, Thai Dragon, Rooster Spur, Habanero, Cubanelle, and bells without name, yellow, red, purple, green. The first celery. Cornichons and long Armenian cucumbers, Burpless. Then artichokes, a few.

By the Second Birthday, After Frost (Wayne's): Brussels sprouts, each day. Cabbages, late broccoli, flags of leek, mostly King Richard. Puntarelle from seed bought in Rome, eaten with anchovies from Greece. Black Spanish radishes. Carrots, pulled from the ground now until winter freezes. Again, beets. Late lettuces, now Arctic King, Reine des Glaces, Winter Marvel, and Brun d'Hiver—chilly names, but the plants last until snows obscure them, and then are still there in spring. Pumpkins, Rouge vif d'Etampes, Cheese and white Lunette, scarlet Kuri, squash and pumpkin both. Roots now, too, late turnips and black radishes, celeriac, main-crop potatoes, last beets, and carrots. Chicories to force in peat for witloofs.

And then, winter: Nothing harvested now that was not gathered in to store, refrigerator, freezer, and root cellar, now taking the place of garden rows and earth. In cool sand, carrots, beets, black radishes, turnips, and celeriac. In boxes of earth, celery, Brussels sprouts, leeks. Deep in peat, chicories swelling. Cabbages piled beneath burlap, their own decaying leaves a humid protective wrap for hearts solid until spring. Pumpkins piled in spaces heated for human comfort, but barely, halls, odd corners of the house, such places. Tomatoes, vivid still in jars, now rich with good oil, with garlic and herbs.

Missing from this litany is sweet corn, the great queen of high-summer gardens and, for most Americans, the emblem, almost the synecdoche, of the season in which it comes. We grew no corn for many years, because the coons, apparently as comfortable living on this bit of land as are we (though we have never actually seen one), vied with us for the harvest, tasting every ear before it was ripe, leaving us only the ruined stalks and shredded ears as proof of their premature degustation. But we missed everything about corn—the satisfyingly large seed, so easy to drill into neat rows; the beauty of the emerging shoots and young plants, textured like nothing else one grows in a vegetable garden, quickly making walls of rich green; the ceremony of cooking, when the ears are judged ripe, the huge pot boiling, the trek to the garden, the picking and the sprint back, a bare five minutes passing between the ear's growing and its appearance on the table; the hot butter, the way the kernels burst against the teeth and stay there . . . To have all that again, we have been willing to string electric wires from the fence that contains the cows, one hot wire across the meadow, and a grid around the corn patch. It is laborious work, and the effect is both ugly and (when bare legs brush against the wires) physically unsettling. Still, we once again have our share of ears, and corn has returned to the litany.

As full of plenitude as this list of plants seems to be, it is nevertheless true that the vegetable garden is only a small section of our much larger garden; perhaps as much as seven acres are under intense cultivation. It has many other parts—a formal perennial garden, an allee of roses, deep, bordering boundary beds, a stream garden, a rhododendron walk, a conifer collection, a rock garden, and two greenhouses—in which we grow many other plants besides vegetables. For a garden as cold as ours, we manage to grow all sorts of things, indeed, anything that will survive winters that routinely reach −20° Fahrenheit, and sometimes even lower temperatures. The list of trees, shrubs, vines, perennials, alpines, bulbs, tender shrubs, and greenhouse plants that flourish here surprises even us, though we know for certain that we have bought, propagated, planted, and tended every one. But the garden is not merely a collection of plants, or so we hope. After twenty years of hard work and steady expansion, it seems now an entity, almost a living organism, with its own integrity and its own laws of organization. Giving up any part of it would not be easy for us, for no matter how cunningly we tried to disguise a curtailment, something would feel missing, some part or limb that should be there, absent. So we work hard to stay fit, and at this lucky time we have not had to face the prospect of any sacrifice. Rather, we continue to increase the garden, less by further expansion into the woods that surround it than by consolidation, making part fit tighter into part and increasing the logic and the pleasure of getting from here to there.

We know, however, that if we were forced to it, we would abandon all the parts of the ornamental garden before we surrendered the little patch that feeds us most of the year, snug now in its place at the head of the new meadow. If the rest of the garden had to return to nature, the results would still be beautiful. Here in the cool mountains of southern Vermont, native greenery is lush, and the deep soils we have cultivated and

❧ *Vegetable gardens, more than any other form of garden except formal parterres (to which they are closely allied), seem to demand the order of strict geometry. Here, in very early spring, the fat seeds of broad beans are lined out in the cold earth, rather more closely together than most crops, as they are nitrogen-fixing and seem to flourish best when crowded together. A guiding line created by a bamboo pole pressed into the soft soil might have made for an even more regular arrangement of the seed.*

enriched would give even better starts to the maples, beeches, oaks, and hemlocks that would quickly reforest our small clearing. Such exotics as could comfortably survive the deepening shade—rhododendrons, fothergillas, some viburnums, many groundcovers, the small bulbs—might still persist, leaving the native flora richer and offering a memory of the garden that was once here. The results, though a ruin, to be sure, would still be evocative, and in their way a fit setting for our last decade here.

But giving up the vegetable garden would mean that we would cease to eat. We would continue to put food in our mouths, we suppose, though certainly we can both imagine states of loss and depression so grave as to make even that minimal effort at survival pointless. But at this time of our lives, the ingestion of food merely for the purpose of survival is not what we mean by eating. To be nourished directly from a garden for years and years, to become accustomed not only to the tastes but also to the labors and rituals it offers, the small festivals, makes even the fanciest gourmet market seem thin. Corn is not the only crop that, eaten as soon after harvest as possible, surprises even memory with what it can be. Carrots taste both sweeter and of the earth when eaten just pulled, their flavor rusty with minerals. Peas need no butter, no cooking, even. Baby potatoes the size of marbles can be bought in no market, golden purslane and orach in only a few. In the door of no market that we know of can ripening tomatoes be smelled as we smell them in August when the garden gate swings open. Artichokes, which we grow here with great effort, are tender and sweet, without the ferrous taste and fibrous chew that marks store-bought ones. From each plant we may coax two or three apple-sized buds before frosts come to remind us where we live. From two long rows of fava beans we can pick at most only two or three company-sized servings. From as many rows of butter beans, sadly less.

Giving up the growing of vegetables would entail other sacrifices as well, not at the table but

❧ *Vegetable gardens, rightly viewed, are much more than food factories. They are magic places, little worlds set apart from other domestic or horticultural concerns, realms of peace and order. Therefore, approaching them through a special gate ought to signal a change of mood, a lightening and gladdening of the spirit.*

Harvest

in our lives as gardeners. For among all the other forms of gardening we practice, the raising of vegetables has its own rhythms, its own curious pleasures. Vegetable gardens are orderly affairs, both regulated and regulating. More than any other form of gardening, they are dependent on system and pattern and on time. Elsewhere in the garden, one often has a window of a month or two, sometimes more, to accomplish what one dreams of. Bulbs, for example, can be planted whenever they arrive in early autumn (if our orders have been prompt) in weather that seems still like summer; but they can wait in their paper bags through the glorious turning of the leaves, and may even be planted (as is too often the case here) with frozen fingers in the rime-crusted ground of early November. Perennials, at least in zone 4, are best established in spring, because autumn planting will subject the shallow crowns to heaving and thawing throughout mild spells in winter, popping them out of the ground like corks. Still, spring is a very long season in southern Vermont, and so the work may be done almost as early as the ground thaws in April, though May and even early June will serve as well. Deciduous shrubs and new trees can be planted in spring or fall, or indeed (if they are bought as canned specimens) any time during the growing season. But the work of planting vegetables must be done on time, and time is often short.

Peas, for example, if sown after July 1, will never bear, at least not here, no matter how cool and wet late summer may be. Corn sown in cold earth will never sprout in compliance with our impatience, and so the fat, wrinkled seed must be drilled just when the weather becomes settled and dry, usually somewhere around the tenth of June. Fava beans, if we are to have them at all, must be planted as early as possible, when the soil is still winter-cold and unpleasantly wet to work. But artichokes are seeded as early as February and grown in the basement under lights, so that when they are planted out, they are already mature plants, tricked into flowering by the still cool nights of early summer. Some crops, such as radishes and spinach, are sown to mature before the full heat of summer causes them to bolt, and others, such as beans, will mature only then. A few, chiefly cabbages and their kin, will require the longest season possible, becoming most flavorful only when they have been mellowed by the bitterness of late autumn. Time matters more in a vegetable garden than in any other, and so the maturation periods of crops are stamped on the seed packet to the day—30, 78, 120, and so forth. But at any season, one day is not equal to another, and so against these numbers we must put our knowledge of the movement of the sun, the steady increase and then decrease of hours of light in proportion to hours of darkness.

Whenever time is under strict regulation, a certain formality seems to occur. So vegetable gardens are generally rather formal, with crops grown in neat rows and patterns on the ground. For years, that was as far as we got in vegetable garden design. The vegetable plot (and there has been one here, for twenty years) has moved about the property, generally occupying whatever space of ground was about to be developed, the next year or the year after that, as part of the purely ornamental garden. Our first summer after the house was built, it was established square in the backyard. Or rather, what was eventually to be the backyard, since at that time we looked out only on a waste of fearfully disturbed soil, compacted by the bulldozer's attempt to make it reasonably smooth and level. Shovels were useless to break it up. A pickax was required. We did what we could to make the soil more friable by

❧ *In the design of a vegetable garden, vertical structures are terribly important, for many garden crops such as potatoes, bush beans, lettuce, and the like form horizontal planes upon the ground. Peas, pole beans, and tomatoes are treasured, then, because they must be grown aloft, and providing for their comfort allows one also to create structures that are at once as useful as they are beautiful.*

hauling buckets of decomposed leaves from the forest floor, and we mulched each row heavily with spoiled hay. (In fact, we have never grown better tomatoes than we did that year, though they were simple catalog orderings with the word "boy" or "girl" in their names. The rich world of heirloom tomatoes lay yet before us, as before most people.) After a winter of mellowing and with all the amendments we had added, the soil looked decent. But no more vegetables were to profit from it. It was raked smooth, and seeded to grass, and the vegetable plot was moved behind the newly planted yew hedge that was eventually to form the north boundary to the perennial garden.

Not that the perennial garden was then a thought in our minds, for we had not begun to see even that far. The hedge was planted, actually, with the expectation that it would separate the vegetable garden from the new lawn, where we supposed it would stay for as long as we gardened here. In the beginning, it was not much of a hedge, either, but only a straight line of evenly spaced three-foot-high bushes, with a gap between each and its neighbor. Still, its approximate eighty feet of length provided one side of a rough rectangle, and we were delighted at how the firm barrier of the incipient hedge, more psychological than actual, contributed order to the space, though it remained open on the other three sides. For a year or two, only tall corn provided enclosure and privacy on the side bordering the public road, but both ends were open. One looked toward our neighbor's pasture and barns, and the other to what now seems a surprisingly vast front yard, with little evergreen trees planted in it that eventually became the back layer of the deep shrubbery border that now screens the front of our property.

Primitive as it was, that second vegetable garden became our first flirtation with the concept of garden rooms, for it was divided off from the rest of the property, and within, it had its own special character and charm, albeit only of neat, orderly rows, healthy food plants and raked dirt paths. Almost by instinct rather than by conscious design, we increased the sense of enclosure, first by planting four whips of antique apples at the top, thus providing some sense of separation from the pasture above but still leaving a glimpse of the fine barns in the distance. (So naive were we then that the little trees were planted along the property line, which was not at a right angle to the hedge. Two years later, when light dawned, they were dug up and replanted.) Still, however, we remained open on two sides, along the road and toward the lawn on the south end.

At that time in the garden's history, an accident occurred that influenced both that space and eventually the garden as a whole. Soils here in southern Vermont are mostly very good—a deep, sandy clay loam generally enriched, where it has not been disturbed, with humus from tended pastures or from woodland. But it is glacial till, and so each thrust of the shovel is apt to turn up stones, most of which can be lifted or rolled away, but a few of which may require half a day of sweating labor to budge. Old Vermonters say that the soil here grows stones, for that is

the easiest way to explain why patiently cleared and cultivated land will still, each spring, produce a new crop of them. In fact, they seem to rise by alternate freezing and thawing from levels deeper than shovel or plow can reach, up to the point where they cannot be ignored and must be dealt with. In the development of this second vegetable garden, we hit one at every thrust, and until they could be carted away, they were piled at the end of the space where the yew hedge stopped.

The idea that came next was obvious enough, though we could little have guessed at the days and years of excruciating labor we had taken on. We decided to use our stones to build a wall, enclosing the southern and eastern sides of the garden. We little knew, then, where this casual impulse would lead us, for the building of walls became a sort of passion, though (like many others in life) our first efforts were so clumsy that we wonder now how it could have taken such a hold on us. At first it was just something to do with the stones, and a way, as we dug, of turning an annoyance into a moment of joy, a sort of treasure hunt that lightened the labor of digging.

There is much besides beauty to recommend a wall. It is free for only the labor, at least here, and the results, in some form or another, will last forever. The exercise is good for the body, and the mind delights in the visible results of each day's labor. When a particular day seems right for the work, there comes, too, after an hour or so of warm-up, a synchrony of hand and mind beneath conscious thought that is matched only by a perfect stint at weeding. Without thinking, the mind notes a gap between stones, a void to fill, and the hand selects just the one stone from the pile that will perfectly fill it. Few things are as satisfying as the clear *tock* that indicates the perfect seating of a stone against its neighbors.

Then a new void is opened, a new stone selected to fill it, and the work progresses through a long and peaceful afternoon. If all the other necessities of one's life comply, it is good to do a bit of this work every day, though the great trick, in the almost narcotic state it produces, is to stop just in time to be able to go back to the work the day after. Approached in this way (which is to say, incrementally), a wall progresses by sections, each becoming a visible and almost eternal proof of how one has spent one's day.

There is no guidebook we know of that can teach the building of a wall. Those who have the aptitude can learn by working with someone who knows how to do it, though one must ask very few questions, learning simply by fetching the stones from the pile, watching them accepted or rejected, fitted snugly into place or tossed aside for future use. Lacking a good teacher (as we were stupid to have done in the beginning), one simply must learn from the work itself, and the first results, like as not, will hardly be a thing to be proud of. We began in autumn, and made slow progress. Winter came before hardly eighteen feet of wall had been completed, and the following spring, winter's freezing and thawing had caused the ground to buck off our work, so that the only distinction between our first section of wall and the waiting pile of rock was that the first was in a more or less straight line and the second in a rounded heap. But all through the second summer, we got better and better, learning the uses of stones—as face rock or dead man or chink or cap; how to spot a fault line made when two or three courses of stone failed to overlap, and mostly, to know by instinct when a stone had not locked firmly into its place, but was merely balanced there, subject to tumbling by a slight shift in the earth and the inexorable laws of gravity. Perhaps one best learns to build a wall by rebuilding a wall, or at least we did, and by the third summer, we had succeeded in surrounding the south and east sides of the garden with a four-foot-high wall of passable quality and had even begun extending it across the west end against our neighbor's pasture, bringing the apple trees, which before had seemed to float there, firmly within its boundaries.

What resulted was a perfectly defined space within which the growing of vegetables took on quite a new meaning. For now the rows started and stopped for clear reasons, and cunning little beds could be made down the middle, edged with alpine strawberries. But though our interest in growing vegetables steadily increased, so did our interest in other branches of horticulture. Fickle as we were to our first love, the space we had created seemed too pretty for vegetables, and so it was turned into a garden of perennials and roses in deep beds against the walls and hedge, with a rectangular panel of lawn where the strawberry-edged squares had been. The vegetables were banished, for the third time, to the frontier of a garden now rapidly developing.

Specifically, we established a new vegetable garden below the drive, in what was then an exhausted strip of old meadow bordered on the south side by the public road and on the north by unthinned woodland of maple, beech, black cherry, and hemlock. The growth of weeds and straggling grasses and brambles that clothed the space was dreadfully thin, and the soil, once plowed up, proved to be the worst on the property. Everything good in it appeared to have been stripped away at some time in the distant past, leaving only thin sandy clay and gravel. Later, a very old neighbor told us that she had walked the road as a small child when it was hardly more than a dirt path, and that some time in the thirties topsoil from our bit of meadow had been

❧ *We thought our second vegetable garden beautiful enough, and it was full of play. Perhaps its most important contribution to the development of all our gardens, however, was that we learned, slowly at first, better with time, how to build walls, and more, how important it was to set off sections of the garden into individual rooms, each with its own resonance, its own special purpose and charm.*

❦ *Even for us, who have watched the space evolve over twenty years, it is still hard to imagine that our perennial garden was once planted to rows of beans and corn and cabbage. Still, over time any garden becomes a palimpsest, allowing one to read beneath its present surface all that was and even perhaps will be, when one's own tenure in it is at an end. When we sit here on a rare late June evening, we can still imagine the beds of alpine strawberries, and even the joy of picking them. What will come after—we confess it—is a little harder to imagine.*

The space once occupied by our third vegetable garden is now an expanse of lawn, a rockery, and a conifer border shielding against the traffic of the road, such, in this remote country town, as it is. Whatever beauty it now possesses is much enhanced by the tilling, manuring, and fertilizing of the soil for the vegetable crops it once supported, and more, for the knowledge we gained while working the rows, of light patterns, the tilt of the earth, prevailing winds, and the essential nature of the space.

carted over—together with, ironically, an old stone wall—to make the bed for an asphalt road. We would have given almost anything for that wall (which, over the years, we have put back), but we would have given even more for the good soil on which the road now rested. Still, we had proved twice that "poor" soils are often rich in minerals, and with the addition of humus can be made to support vegetable crops. So we ordered in mountains of manure from a neighboring dairy farm, hauled more buckets of leaf mold from the woods, and mulched heavily with more spoiled hay, not only to add additional organic

matter but also to keep the thin soil from caking and cracking in summer.

The garden we established there was nothing like its predecessor, in either productivity or attractiveness. For one thing, it was too big. The whole slope, some three hundred feet long and a hundred feet wide, was ours, and we felt somehow that we should plant the whole thing, end to end and side to side. Not all was vegetables, for we quickly found that they would not thrive beneath the bordering edge of woodland trees, all dense of shade and greedy for moisture. So a nursery was established along that edge, planted to cuttings of ornamental shrubs, stock plants of hostas, and the first two parents of the *Primula japonica* that have since naturalized by thousands along the stream.

Still there were too many vegetables, both to tend and to eat. Rows and rows of them straggled down the slope, broken occasionally—not for aesthetic reasons but to prevent erosion—by rows across. Nothing motivated us then but the desire to plant as much of everything as we could. We assumed that the weeding, staking, harvesting (freezing and canning) would somehow take care of itself. It didn't, of course, for we both were schoolteachers then, with very short summers; and the garden, so trim and tidy when it was freshly planted in spring and grew into early summer, was, by August, a tangle of weeds and an overplus of overripe and unusable food.

The worst thing about that space, however, was that it had no clear boundaries, no frame. The unthinned woodland (for ten years now our rhododendron garden) provided us with one firm edge, and it was pretty to look up from weeding to its wall of leaf. But the space was open at the top toward the drive, and worse, exposed along the road, causing us to spend more time waving to passing cars than to weeding. (One waves to all passing cars, here in Vermont.) We struggled with a hedgerow of deciduous flowering shrubs and trees along that road, though they rooted shallowly and grew poorly in the thin soil, and once, in a dry, strong wind of May, we watched a large hawthorne in full leaf and flower snap off at its base and blow away. Mostly, that garden was a mess, though we had fun with it, and on some level we knew what we were learning and what we were up to.

Eventually, it became apparent to us that our third vegetable garden would have to go the way of its predecessors. Though we tended it as well as we could, we had begun to realize that it would never be much more than a homely affair, however productive. By its third year of existence (our eighth here) the soils had become—through the addition of a staggering amount of cow manure, leaf duff, and spent hay—good enough to support some other form of horticulture. And other forms were then principally what we had in mind, as our sophistication about plants grew— doubtless our greed, too—and our sense that we were not merely cultivating plants, but actually making a garden on a rather grand scale.

We had been looking at that bordering wood for three years of sowing, weeding, and harvesting, and it slowly occurred to us that it was suitable for better things than merely to shelter our Scots Highland cows. Within its scrappy understory of second- and third-growth maples and brushy hemlocks was a rhythm of magnificent towering ash trees, by twos from the same root (as they often grow) and singly. There was a splendid old black cherry, too crooked of trunk to make it worth the harvesting when the land was last logged in the thirties, and several large maples that had developed branches sweeping the ground where the light at the woodland edge had let them. Best of all, our stream, which we had begun to develop above, had cut a dramatic channel through the woods, providing (or so we thought then) a logical boundary to a woodland garden. We had not at that time done much with shade gardening, having concentrated on border perennials and vegetables, but by then we had come to know Linc and Timmy Foster, and their beautiful garden, Millstream, in Falls Village, Connecticut, had shown us what might be possible. Then too, we had become aware of the work David Leech had done on rhododendrons, creating beautiful cultivars far hardier than the few

Dexter hybrids we had struggled with. So that side of the space took on a new identity in our minds, and at that time (perhaps since) any idea we had about the garden had to become reality.

There was the problem, too, of the road. By then we had successfully screened it from view in the perennial garden by planting a loose grove of arborvitae within the wall, and they had grown so quickly that cars and horses passed without notice, and without a wave. The small pines in the front yard had also increased in size to fifteen feet and had become, with a thickening of Serbian and Colorado spruce, the backbone of a forty-foot-deep border, faced on the lawn side with small deciduous trees—a Sargent crab, a flowering cherry ('Hally Jolivette'), a Washington thorn and a 'Snowbank' crab apple. We luxuri-ated in all this privacy, and we wanted more. So the failed hedgerow that attempted to secure it along the road side of the vegetable garden was grubbed up, and the bordering ground planted to a collection of large and dwarf conifers. What had been the growing rows was smoothed out and seeded to grass, to form our largest lawn, a sweep of green that descended to what later became the rock garden, bog, and working greenhouse.

We should say here, parenthetically, that it is a very good thing, in the development of a gar-den, to treat the garden for growing vegetables as an outrider, a scout of unknown territories. Each of our first three vegetable gardens, however temporary their presence on our land and how-ever clumsy their design, served us, nevertheless,

The present rhododendron garden was once the bordering edge of our third vegetable garden. In the patient weeding we did among that garden's carrots, we looked over our shoulder and saw what might be there. It is there now, though the carrots, so help-ful in their capacity to focus images of the future, have moved on.

very well. They provided food, of course, and they taught us how to bring crops to fruition, which varieties to choose, how to sow and tend, weed and fertilize. More, they taught us the management of soils, the best ways to husband what we were given and to increase fertility, whether to grow new vegetables or (as was the case) flowers, lawns, and ornamental shrubs and trees. We learned a great deal, too, in each space, about patterns of light and shade, prevailing winds, pockets of warmth and frost, all very useful knowledge for creating the gardens they have since become. Something was learned, too, about the textures of leaves and growing stalks and the characters of plants, for vegetables are very beautiful, and one quickly perceives that certain combinations are deeply satisfying, and others a lost chance, put in place merely because the row was open and the seed packet in one's hand. Most of all, however, we learned about design, about how garden rooms could be fashioned with clear defining walls, each with its own special character, its own pleasures and surprises. Those are all lessons that vegetable gardening teaches, with surprising directness and clarity, if one is ready to learn. Before describing the next vegetable garden, however (the fourth and next to last), we should say that many of these lessons were still sinking in, not yet actually operative and ready to bear fruit. Though vegetables were gone from the area below the drive, they were hardly banished from our life. Their next home came to be perhaps one of the greatest follies we have perpetrated here, and in some ways one of the most delightful.

Our property, though it is only twenty-six acres, seems much larger because it is shaped like a key, the narrow part running deep into the woods. At its very tip is a beautiful little meadow of perhaps three or four acres, sloping south and

❧ *The fourth of our vegetable gardens at North Hill occupied part of a meadow deep in the woods at the back of the property. It was a distinctly baggy-pants affair, suggesting, in its monotonous rows, pioneer subsistence farming in the wilderness. Still, it was a peaceful place, made more so by the companionable presence of our cows.*

bordered on three sides by deep woods and on the fourth by a very old apple orchard. That we own it at all is the accident of old deeds— deaths, divorces, and sometimes desperate sales of land—that caused our bit to be carved up in a rather curious fashion. The meadow is approached from the house by a quiet lane through the woods, an old logging road, actually, and one breaks into its sunlight after a gentle, uphill walk of perhaps a quarter of a mile. It was there that we thought to establish the fourth vegetable garden, as well as an extensive nursery of perennials, shrubs, and trees that we intended to propagate for eventual use in the ornamental gardens below.

Actually, very many things recommended the spot. It was beautiful, completely sheltered by its surrounding woods from view and from harsh winds. The south-facing slope caused cold air to drain away, ensuring an extra frost-free week or more at each end of the growing season, precious when the whole of it was scarcely more than 120 days. Sometime in the early forties, the meadow had been patiently stoned and plowed up to grow potatoes. But for almost fifty years it had been used to graze cows, which kept it clear of brush and enriched its soil, so that we could turn up friable earth two shovelfuls deep. Best of all, about twenty yards into the woods was an old, stone-lined well, originally the source of drinking water for a farmhouse far below. Now unused and capped by a rusty sheet of iron, it had, in the earliest memory of our neighbors, never run dry. Though the water was probably not of drinking quality, buckets could still be dipped into it to water young seedlings and newly transplanted crops.

So we set to work, hiring a plowman to turn and level a rectangular space at the top, perhaps two hundred feet long and eighty feet deep. By then we owned a Rototiller, a foolish and noisome tool that we have since dispensed with, but it was handy for churning up clumps of sod and for the work (absurd, but something we then thought necessary) of re-making the rows each year. As with the garden before, so much space was at our command that we exercised no judgment about what we planted, or how much of it. So vast was that garden, and so demanding, that it seems to us now we did little else but work there, weeding, hoeing, fertilizing, and harvesting, all summer long. That could not have been the case, actually, for the ornamental gardens around the house continued to develop, and they must have taken much of our time in summer. Still, we remember long days when we left for the garden early in the morning, carrying up a lunch and drinking water, and spent all the time between first light and last working there, wearing Speedo bathings suits, or less if the day was very warm.

That space had great advantages over the one before. Its soils were deep and rich, and it had clear boundaries on all sides. Behind it and to one side was the woods, and the apple orchard framed the other. Across its front, a sturdy fence reserved the rest of the meadow for the cows and kept them out of what was ours. (They were mostly there in summer, lazing in the shade or standing stolidly just at the fence, waiting expectantly for buckets of weeds or spent crops; they were good companions, never jangling our labor with silly chatter.) The space was private and peaceful, and so far from the house that no phone calls, no casual impulse for a soda or a piece of fruit, could interrupt the long days of work, once we were settled to them. So what one expects most from gardening on a spiritual level, a deep sense of peaceful solitude, was richly available in that spot, and actually, we came to miss much of that after the vegetable garden was moved for its last time.

Its greatest advantage, the very thing that had made it so wonderful, proved in the end to make it impossible. It was simply too far from where we dwelled. "Rather too far, *I* should think," Christopher Lloyd commented, "for a handful of parsley." But it wasn't just parsley. We could plan ahead for that, at day's end, or do without, or keep a huge clay pot with it thriving, as we did, close to the kitchen door. And if we had not brought down what we needed at the close of a day's labor, we rather liked the brisk trot back, for beans or

❧ *On a densely wooded property the cutting of trees is always a painful business, for they are often as old or much older than oneself, and beautiful, and they cannot be put back, once down. Still, felling them is perhaps best thought of as the breaking of eggs to make a cake. Actually, we had no idea when our small meadow was cleared that it would be our fifth and final vegetable garden. But any passionate gardener, given a space in which to do something, will sooner or later do something. Now, by a process of illogic known to all gardeners, what is there seemed inevitable and entirely intended from the first.*

radishes or corn, not just because it was one more chance, at twilight, to visit that enchanted spot, but also (or so we kept saying then) because the exercise was good for us, doubling the benefit of the fresh produce we went after.

The great problem was that the garden was essentially too far away to make its maintenance possible. A handful of herbs is one thing, or a bucket of beans. But the hard slog up with a fifty-pound bag of lime or two brim-full buckets of 5-10-10 was quite another. We had a four-wheel-drive truck (have it still), but after a trip or two in one wet spring, the vehicle mired deep in a wet spot, a would-be stream, and it took half a

day of hard and hopeless labor to free its wheels from the sodden woodland soil. It was never driven up that way again. And at the last harvest, on a chilly evening at twilight when all the instruments agreed that a black frost was certain and the garden needed to be stripped of everything savable—squash and pumpkins, ripe and green tomatoes, eggplants, any last beans, bouquets of basil and other herbs, celery and celeriac—so many trips down with a wheelbarrow and up again became almost a metaphysical question about the meaning of life.

So after five years, the decision was made to move the vegetable garden yet again, to what we assume will be the place it will be forever, or at least forever in any sense of the word applicable to us. The previous space was abandoned, and the barrier fence pulled down, to the immense delight of the cows. For the grass there is (and always will be) richer than in any other part of their pasture, and there is a surprise for them, though it grows weaker and weaker each year, in the tender asparagus that sprouts from a wide bed we had thought would always be for our exclusive use. A very fine specimen of *Rosa rugosa* 'Blanc double de Coubert' still flourishes there, too spiny for their tastes and looking rather nice amidst the browsed grass. There are a few hardy boxwoods, one 'Festiva Maxima' peony, and a small patch of *Pulmonaria caerulea,* unobvious except in spring, when it is an odd contrast of vivid sky blue against the vernal green of the grass. We go up there now at most two or three times in a summer, to check the fences and to guide our lovesick bull away from the ladies he knows are waiting, far across the distant fields. Otherwise, the meadow is as it was when we came here, a charmed, almost forgotten place, and we have moved on. But we remember the garden that was there, how nice it was, and also how important in our progress toward the vegetable garden we were all along unconsciously creating.

Our last vegetable garden—the one with which we live now in such contentment—had a great deal more help in coming into being than any of the others. First, it occupies a space that we created by deliberate design. Because of the presence of our stream, which is one of the great treasures of the garden and the reason we came to live here, it was impossible to build a house deep in the woods, as we had originally hoped. We could have gotten across, and so could a light vehicle, a car, or even a pickup truck. But cement mixers, well drillers, and trucks delivering heavy

timbers and other building supplies were another matter, and we were told firmly by our builder that we could have either a bridge or a central chimney that offered fireplaces in every room of the house. We opted, of course, for the chimney, thinking that a bridge was a worky sort of thing, but a deep fireplace in the kitchen was pure romance. We are not sorry, though it meant that our house had to be built rather close to the road, leaving the deep woods for other uses.

For two or three years, absorbed as we were by house building and by our first simple attempts at gardening, we left the woods alone. They were fine enough, as no logging had occurred in them for more than fifty years. Among mature beeches and maples were even larger trees that had been passed over, either because they had grown in ways that would have made them poor choices for timber, or because they were sugar maples that could be counted on to yield an annual crop for syrup. So among thick stands of second- and third-growth timber were splendid old trees, some of which were three hundred years old. But the beauty of the woods was obscured by an understory of smaller trees, congested and thickety, poor of growth because of overcrowding, with dim futures before them as mature trees. The wall of the woods also pressed on us, stopping the eye and making our property seem much smaller than it in fact was. By then we had met Jim Sprague, an old neighbor now dead, who was—among all his other distinctions—a great woodsman. We entered with him into an agreement to thin the woods above the house and to clear a meadow of three or so acres on its other side, so that one would look through noble old trees to a clearing of light. In return for the labor, he agreed to take half the wood, leaving us the rest for our new fireplaces. The open space that would result would have, we felt, some wonderful use later on, we didn't know exactly what.

Thinning a wood is an exciting business. One moves through, studying the form and placement of each tree carefully, its species and probable future, its individual beauty, both as it is and as it can be expected to become. Choices are sometimes hard, when two fine trees are too close together and one must go, or when the best are all of one species, maples or beeches, but one lone oak or golden birch offers diversity and the promise of seedlings of its own kind. (We know that we cut down one huge basswood, the only one we have ever seen hereabouts, because it was in the wrong place and we didn't know what it was.) In our clearing, we proceeded according to principles just exactly the contrary to those practiced by a good woodsman, for we left the oldest trees, sound or not, and eliminated the youngest. That was very poor wood management, Jim thought, but he had a respect for old living things, and he shrewdly realized that our concerns were only for our own future pleasure, and not for anybody else's mere profit. The results of that thinning are now, after twenty years, very beautiful. Great old boles of beech and maple rise up with unobstructed splendor, and a woodland path curves among them, going from the pergola walk to the poultry house. In the woodland litter beneath them, fifteen thousand chionodoxa have been planted, making waves of blue in early spring, our first great show.

There is no pleasure, by contrast, in clear-cutting, except perhaps that of seeing the sky open above, and having a place to stand and breathe. It is generally a brutal business, and one must simply be ruthless, turning away from any thought of the magnificence of any particular tree, its age or form or relative scarcity as a species among others. All must go down. We waffled only once, when a hundred-year-old golden birch, thickly buttressed at its roots as old trees of that species are, attracted our love, though it was too far out from the defined edge of the clearing. "Cut it down," Jim said. "It is at the end of its life." "Leave it," the softer of us replied. "Let's see." So Jim turned away, though later he built a brush pile under it for burning, from which it took five years to recover. But it is there still, after the twenty years in which he went from a hale seventy-year-old to ninety, and we made a similar (but not, at least superficially, so dramatic) progress along the same road. He is dead now, but the tree is thriving, having gotten, it appears, a whole new lease on life from the thinning around it, and perhaps, the rich deposit of tree ash at its roots. It will probably outlive us as well.

For some years, our new cleared space was a fairly scrappy thing, before stumps rotted away and burn piles healed over. Woodland soils are not always rich, sometimes being merely a thin overspread of humus and decaying leaves on rocky clay soils. That was the case with ours, and only scant vegetation came at first: mosses, andropogons and other lean-living grasses, heath asters, and brambles. Bit by bit, however, as tree roots and stumps rotted and herbaceous material decayed, the soil became richer, able to support goldenrods and taller asters and of course more brambles. After seven years or so, the space became quite pretty, and we had gained enough knowledge to recognize just what it was after all intended for, though we could hardly have known when the work was first undertaken to clear it. We decided that the spot, pleasantly framed by the woods and possessing its own identity (though not at such a daunting distance from the kitchen door), was exactly the place to give our very peripatetic vegetable garden its final location.

By then we knew a great deal about soils, and over the years we had also achieved some firm convictions about design. Even a glance at our clearing, now something like a meadow, showed rocks and large, partially buried boulders studding its extent. It had never been stoned for farming, and the presence of those rocks at the surface promised many, possibly very many, beneath. It sloped as well, as does all our land here in the mountains, though the incline was gradual, not hopeless of leveling. As vegetable gardens are largely formal things—and as we wanted ours to be very formal, with many cunning structures of beds and fruiting plants—we knew that we needed a space as level as possible. So we engaged a young bulldozer operator, staked out a perfect rectangle at the top of the clearing that measured eighty feet across its face and sixty feet deep, and wished him luck. He shook his head.

We then had to be away for three days, a good thing for us and for him, given the frustrations he faced. We returned home just as he was loading his machine in the public road, and he said, "I hope you like what I have done," and left. Immediately we went up to the space and found it as perfectly level as we could wish, banked gently where it faced the slope of the meadow. And behind, against the woodland edge, was a magnificent stone wall extending the full length of the rectangle, in a gently curving arc, made of enormous rocks, one locked neatly into the other. Like it? We were thrilled. It was, in a most unusual positive sense, far more than we had bargained for. When we called with our congratulations and to settle our bill, the young man said, "Well, I'm glad you're pleased; I had to do *something* with all those ugly rocks."

One more thing was needed, or perhaps two, to complete our splendid new vegetable garden.

By then we had become firm believers in enclosure, in structures that defined spaces clearly and created garden rooms. By chance, we had been given the name of a man in central Vermont who still harvested native locust and split it by hand in the old way. So we arranged to have our new space defined by a split-rail fence, in the most antique manner, which quickly weathered to a gentle gray and provided space to espalier dwarf apple trees. Our efforts at training them were at first clumsy, and the results will never look like the scaffold of an ancient pear tree from the seventeenth century that we once saw in Paris, in the gardeners' common room at the Jardins du Luxembourg, preserved as a sort of textbook of how that work was perfectly to be done. Still, after three years our young trees are taking on a reasonably respectable shape, and they provide extra thickness to the fence in summer and great beauty in winter when they are bare.

The only other thing that remained to have was a poultry house. We had begun our life together on Boston's Beacon Street (number 89), across from the Public Garden. There we kept ornamental poultry in cages. The great, high-ceilinged ballroom we inhabited made very improbable surroundings for fluffy white Cochins, Old English game cocks, spangled Mille Fleurs, pheasants, and quail. (Fortunately, it was an old neighborhood, fairly inured to eccentricities of all sorts.) We came to love their variety, their cheerful sounds, their splendid patterns of feather, and their tiny, cunning bodies. Through our first fifteen years in Vermont we had missed them, though we had no place here to make them comfortable. Now we did, and so a small poultry house, of raw pine that has now weathered gray like the fence, was built at the north edge of the garden, attached to it, and peopled with many breeds and with three pairs of com-

The conviction that all garden spaces should be enclosed comes slowly; but when it comes, no open edges, no dribbling off into other things, is tolerable. When our new vegetable garden came to be enclosed by a split-rail locust fence, we knew then where it was and where it stopped and where other things began. A greater order became possible, because rows and quadrants could be aligned to firm edges and angles, and one could look up and know where the weeding of a row would end. Beyond all that, the vegetable garden became its own world, opening the day with a sense of peace when we came up to release the poultry, and closing it with tranquillity when we harvested for dinner.

panionable geese that now graze the lane up to the vegetable garden.

Within the confines of the fence, beds and rows are set out more or less symmetrically, or at least as symmetrically as we, who cannot go straight, can manage. Little trees, of currant and gooseberry trained as standards, stand in the center of each square bed and draw the eye up off the ground, making the garden seem, for all its practicality, somehow fanciful, like an image in a medieval manuscript, *hortus inclusus,* the garden of paradise. Fruit is everywhere. Strawberries surround little trees of Asian pear and dwarf apricot.

A hedge of raspberries, half bearing gold and half ruby, runs all along the back fence. Highbush blueberries make a hedge along the shaded south side where the poultry house is, as pretty in all seasons as any ornamental shrub in the gardens below. Standard pears and apples, all of antique, half-forgotten varieties, have been planted in the meadow and on the slope above the garden, between the fence and our fine accidental stone wall. Some day they will make great gnarled trees—not in our time, but the thought is still nice.

Though large enough, our present vegetable

❦ *Gardening is always a rather solitary activity, but it is made far less lonely when other living creatures are going about their busy lives, and one can delight them and oneself by small attentions. Sometimes we are not sure whether we cultivate our vegetable garden for ourselves or for our flock of ornamental poultry, but we do know that the addition of a poultry house has immeasurably increased our pleasure in the space.*

❦ *Exotic poultry come in many fantastic shapes. In Japanese phoenix one may have tails five or six feet long, in jungle Sumatras, the inky black of crows, and in crested Polish, feathery topknots as elaborate as the most fanciful Easter bonnet. Still, the chickens we have loved best are fat and rounded in shape, like the French hens in the fairy tales of one's childhood. That being said, we find it hard, when we haunt the great autumn poultry shows, to resist an impulse purchase of a trio of Mille Fleurs, or an Old English porcelain rooster, engagingly cocky for all his diminutive size, with his two tiny, smooth-feathered slaty hens.*

garden is smaller than either of its two immediate predecessors, just the right size, we think, for growing what we like and for creating the pattern on the ground that we must have dreamed of all along. Still, however, we get the familiar question "Why so large a vegetable garden, just for two people?" Well, abundance, both actual and spiritual, is (or ought to be) the mark of any such endeavor. There are always guests and gifts to give in season. Still, we grow more than we can eat or share. We freeze nothing, preferring always to eat according to the seasons. But nothing goes to waste. The chickens are close by, and their names are as resonant, their provenance as exotic, as the vegetables we grow, forming another litany,

pleasant to tell over: Buff Brahma, Chinese Cochin, Mille Fleurs, Aurucana, Sumatra, Yokohama, Indian Silky; rag-bag Sebastopol geese, Buff Embdens, gray Africans; guinea hens too from Africa, pearl and lavender; Helmet pigeons, Checquers. So what we cannot consume of fruit, of lettuce, beans, pea vines, vast zucchini, all goes there.

It is August now. There are currants and gooseberries to preserve, tomatoes to tie up and watch anxiously for the first ripening, potatoes to rob for the smallest, most succulent tubers, cucumbers to take when they are as slender as a finger, the last few pods of peas to eat raw as we gather salads for every meal. It is August, and the garden is paradise.

❧ *All gardens must be at once very serious and very playful, for they represent simultaneously a near approximation of the sublime and also the preservation of the child within us. Vegetable gardens, being, as we would argue, the quintessence of all gardening, preserve both these qualities, or rather, interlock them in a vital way. But in one's seriousness it is easy to lose whimsy, which this funny, lemon-colored chair seems to bring into our garden, wherever it is moved to.*

Harvest

27

❧ *Of all the qualities a vegetable garden must suggest, plenitude, both potential and actual, is the most important. Nothing perhaps could be more depressing, for a gardener at least, than a garden that is thin and meager in its offerings. Never mind that the birds will eat most of the currants, or the chickens most of the beans. It is the thought that counts.*

❧ *It would be presumptuous to suppose that humans, among all living creatures, are alone capable of delighting in many things at once. The redness of some flowers, we have observed, is peculiarly delightful to hummingbirds, though not all red flowers are richest in nectar. It is therefore possible to suppose that supping on something red has, for the hummingbird, an additional pleasure. Certainly it is true that for gardeners, the colors, shapes, and textures of plants provide their own pleasure, not gustatory only, but visual and tactile. The harvest of August, so varied and rich, has therefore many pleasures, though hardly a pod or fruit or berry be eaten.*

Early Spring

♣

Where we live, there is no first day of spring. Thrilling as the idea is, the fact is otherwise; we never lay our heads down on a winter's night to waken the next day into springtime. The metaphor of birth, so often applied and suggesting a sudden alteration from one state to another, a wakening into life, simply isn't the way it is. Rather, spring insinuates itself little by little into the winter and into our awareness, almost like a dye put drop by drop into a glass of water, hardly coloring it at all at first, but eventually, by steady additions, changing its appearance and even its very nature.

For us, the first hint of the coming of spring is in the light, which, in February, subtly alters. February is a month dreaded by many people, a month in which the downward coast of mood that began in December accelerates until it seems to hit bottom. "The only good thing about February," the endlessly repeated adage

❧ *A change in the slant of the light, in early morning and at dusk, is the first sign of spring in southern Vermont. It makes the slog up to the poultry house an event of joy, rather than one more chore to strike off the list. The garden, beyond its fence, still sleeps under a blanket of snow, but we know that it will waken soon enough.*

goes, "is that it is only twenty-eight days long." But for us there is one other good thing; for though the month can be as cold as January (and some years, in its beginning, even colder), though snows lie often at their deepest, February is generally full of light. Clear, bright sunlight floods the house, tempting us to leave our work simply to sit idly in a sunny window. Sunsets again become events worth noting, and can be noted, for in February they begin to occur not while we are still absorbed in our daily work, but after, in the peaceful time when dinner is being gotten ready. Our decision, made some years ago, not to join the rest of the world in October when it shifts to standard time but to hold stubbornly to an extra hour of light at day's end pays hand-

some rewards now. Toward the end of the month, the sun will still be shining at six.

But as eagerly as we note the return of light, we are not the first creatures here to do so. Our flock of pigeons, plump white fantails that have waited out the winter in the loft of the barn, eagerly begin to court. Fantails are not the pigeons preferred by those who breed pigeons for meat, not because they are deficient in quality, but because they are rather small when dressed out. White kings, sturdy, blocky birds as large as a small chicken, are best for that. But our fantails are very beautiful, in a comic sort of way, puffing up their breasts when approached and tucking their heads behind, presumably under the conviction that if they cannot see they also

To the geese, thickly insulated by coats of down and by winter fat, snow is never a problem. Still, even they seem to celebrate the change of the season. Odd and peculiar treasures of our world are the rag-bag Sebastopols, fantastically curled in feather, half pure elegance and half an old barn mop.

cannot be seen. Their courting is comic, too, consisting of much bowing and strutting on the part of the male as he shoulders the hen of his choice into a corner, making all the while the soft, crooning sound that clarifies his intentions. If all goes well, eggs will soon appear, never more than two per pair. But February is still too early in Vermont for successful hatching, since the eggs will freeze solid in the night. Unlike other birds we raise, where a convenient foster mother may be found in the form of a fluffy Cochin hen, pigeons must rear their own young; and should, by some chance, two eggs hatch into pathetic, blind and naked squabs, their parents, at this time of year, will abandon them, with sad consequences.

So during the months of February and March, pigeon eggs are removed from the nest each afternoon and taken for the kitchen. They are of course quite small, never larger than a kumquat, but they are beautiful in shape (as most eggs are) with unusually nacreous shells, as luminous as large pearls. When two eggs have been taken, the pigeon will replace them with two more within a few days. If those are taken in turn, they will again be replaced, and taken again, up to the middle of March, when the weather will become settled enough to make hatching and rearing a safe possibility. Our supply of pigeon eggs is never very abundant, and though they may be used in any way a hen egg could be, we reserve them for special effects—as hard-boiled and pickled additions to a plate of hors d'oeuvres, stuffed (if we have the time and patience), or occasionally fried as a minute "sunny side up" to delight a child.

Though pigeons are our first source of eggs (such as it is) each spring, they are hardly our only supply. Soon the chickens and guineas and geese will also begin to lay again. From late November until the middle of February, we have few fresh eggs. During that period, those we must use, chiefly for baking, come from the supermarket, and we notice the difference. The plenitude of eggs in every market and in every month of the year is the consequence of birds bred to be little more than egg machines. They are kept in quite small cages in heated houses, and fed a precisely calculated ration of food containing the same ingredients (and of course the same hormones) throughout their whole lives (which are brief). The system is not very humane; it also does not produce very good eggs. The lives of our birds contain the whole range of experiences open to a chicken, which, we would actually argue, is fairly large and complicated. In the winter, they reserve their strength to cope with cold and dark, spending their short days searching their litter for specially tasty bits, squabbling a little among themselves, flying to the upper perches and windows to take sunbaths in the wan winter light. It is only when that light increases that they are willing to begin the process of mating and laying (connected activities, obviously, though not for commercial hens), going broody, and setting out a family of chicks. All this is only to say that our chickens and other poultry live real lives, as connected to the seasons as are ours. We are convinced that makes happier chickens. We are certain that it makes better eggs.

The first eggs from the larger poultry begin in February, with the return of light, though if they are laid late in the day, they are apt not to be discovered until early next morning when the birds are fed and watered. By then they will have frozen and cracked, a treat when thawed for the cats or the dog, but not much good for the kitchen. Eggs begin to appear at first by twos and threes, the products of the hardiest, freest-laying hens, the fluffy miniature Cochins; they are either snow white or coal black, and so low to the ground and so fully feathered that they are almost spherical; the stocky bantam Buff Brahmas, which look like the fat French hens of childhood storybooks; the improbably elegant rumpless Aurucanas, kiwi-shaped and many-colored. By the spring solstice, however, the first tentative layers will have been joined by many others, and the laying boxes will be so full that we can carry baskets of eggs to our neighbors. Eggs are the symbol of Easter not only because they are the promise of new life, but also from their sheer abundance then, when they are the first plentiful food of the new year.

Throughout the winter and very early spring, all our birds are gathered together in one great assorted flock. They are confined in the coldest months to an ornamental poultry house at the edge of the vegetable garden, where, with the geese and guineas, their numbers keep them warm. There we slog each morning to carry up fresh water and treats in the form of household scraps and discarded produce from the local co-op market, to vary their diet of grain. When the weather turns and the snows are almost gone, they are freed to range the woods and fields in a colorful wave, as parti-colored as an old-fashioned quilt and as joyfully exuberant as one of Wordsworth's springtime poems.

It is a pleasant peculiarity of humanity that it can take joy from the joy of other species, sharing with them the pleasures they experience, such as the burst of exhilaration that comes with freedom after a long winter of confinement. It may have been that the she-wolf who nursed Romulus and Remus lay before her dark cave taking pleasure in watching their plump, well-fed infant bodies rolling in the warm new grass. We can only guess. But we do know that a lift of the heart occurs in us when the doors of the poultry house are finally thrown open to warm spring sunlight and fresh mud and new grass, and the first, the bravest fowls step across the threshold, cocking their heads in cautious wonder and clucking their assurance to more timid members of the flock.

It is when they are free that the sociology of chickens and the complexity of their system of communication become most apparent. Socially, though they will go about their business in a single flock, they will tend to segregate themselves by breed within it—Cochins with Cochins, Sumatras with Sumatras, Barred Rocks and Brahmas staying close to their own kind. Usually peace obtains, marred only by an occasional squabble between two young cocks more interested in testing their growing prowess than on murderous intent. Their tussles can be comic, as their neck hackles rise, their eyes glower defiantly, and they leap into the air in the manner of kick-boxers. Usually, the fight will be broken up by an older rooster, the current king of the flock, whose rule, though as brief as that of an Aztec monarch, is for the moment absolute. It is true that cockerels and full-grown cocks can fight to the death, in a determined and relentless struggle that usually means the demise of both. Generally, however, that happens only when male birds have been kept separate, outside the common flock, during the long, peaceful winter months. For that reason we try to introduce new adult males only in autumn, and we are vigilant, keeping a wire pen convenient within the poultry house to confine a particularly aggressive bird for a period, in the hope that the humiliation will bring him down a peg or two. Generally, however, a flock of chickens is no more fractious than a human crowd—or, perhaps, much less so.

Over our twenty years of keeping ornamental poultry, we have come to recognize the surpris-

Though their primary sustaining winter diet is cracked corn, the chickens delight in the remains of some good late-winter salad. They are a peaceful flock, good at sharing, though a fine, sheeny black Sumatra hen keeps a discovered olive all to herself.

ingly extensive vocabulary of sounds that chickens can make. Anyone knows the crow of a rooster at dawn, rich in mythological and religious significance, and to us, curiously comforting, one necessary sound among so many of country life. But in a large flock it is a varied sound, no two roosters having quite the same crow, making them recognizable at a distance just from the sounds they make. The smallest birds, Old English gamecocks or Laced Seabrights so tiny that they can be cradled in one's palm, have a high-pitched, metallic-sounding crow, shrill and defiant. From this high note the birds' crowing descends in tone through progressively larger birds to the rich, self-assured voices of the rumpless Aurucanas, the largest birds we keep. (At poultry shows, we have been thrilled by the bass

notes of the giant breeds, standard Cochins and Jersey Giants and the like, whose crows can be as deep and resonant as a steeple bell.) Crows can vary not only in pitch but also in the number of their notes, which is typically four, though sometimes three and sometimes five, as English fairy tales always have it. No matter how many notes, however, there is always a sharp intake of breath after the crow, and the air as it passes over the voice box makes yet another sound, a sort of quiet whistle, which somewhat spoils so proud a performance.

The cackling that celebrates a new-laid egg is less varied, but it turns into a chorus among the flock, all joining in to celebrate the triumph. For most people, a knowledge of the repertory of chickens stops there, though those who attend to their ways will know that they have a much larger vocabulary. Roosters, for example, are very gallant, calling the hens to any specially nice morsel they unearth by a soft crooning sound, and stepping aside while their offering is consumed. Broody hens will voice their objection to being disturbed by a low, gutteral complaint, more a gripe than a warning, and when the tiny chicks hatch, the hens will call to them constantly with a repeated cluck, lest they stray too far. Chickens are great nap takers, too, always resting in the early afternoon, when they make gentle, one-note sounds of contentment deep in their throats, a sort of whirr, their version of a peaceful yawn. When for any reason a bird must be caught, its warning shriek reverberates through the flock, warning of danger, and the sound is picked up and echoed by all the other birds. One would think that courtship would also have its sound, but it begins with a dance instead. An amorous rooster drops his left wing to the ground and holds it tight against his body, fluttering it while stepping sideways, and then mounts the hen of his choice, holding her head firmly in his beak while the brief copulation occurs.

Long ago we came to the conclusion that of all the virtues we might practice, moderation was never to be among them. All our passions have led to excess, and chickens have been no exception. So, though serious breeders will settle on one or at most two breeds, working conscientiously to improve form and feather color, we have, over the years, acquired just about every form of fancy chicken offered. Our flock, therefore, is a motley gathering of many breeds in many shapes, almost a sort of Noah's Ark of chickens, each breed represented by a pair, or sometimes a trio of two hens and a rooster. When the birds have gained strength from their spring-time release, when egg laying is brisk and mating behavior all too apparent, it is time to make choices of those breeds we will allow to produce offspring.

It is always a struggle, for we keep no chickens that are not either very beautiful or eccentrically engaging, and if we had the facilities, we would breed every sort. As it is, we must settle on four, possibly five breeds, since they must be segregated in smaller pens for a month or so. Though all our chickens are bantams, the Aurucanas, Black Sumatras, and Brahmas are all large enough for the table, and so we raise a dozen or so of each breed for that. Despite their Southeast Asian origins, Sumatras are thrifty, hardy birds, able to endure without difficulty the cold of Vermont. It is hard to imagine anything blacker than they are, though in the sunlight, the inky tails of the roosters, low-slung and twice as long as their bodies, have an iridescent emerald sheen. The Aurucanas we keep are of the rumpless sort, with a smooth curve of feather where the tail should be, causing them to look like something prehistoric and extinct. They are descendents of a breed kept by the Aurucana Indians of South America, and among their many peculiarities is the fact that they lay eggs, unique in chickendom, of the pale, bluish-green hue of ancient Chinese celadon porcelain. Brahmas, despite their name, are actually a breed of Colonial American origin, from a cross made very early between Cochins imported from Shanghai and another Colonial breed, apparently now extinct, called Chittagong. The ones we keep are buffs, with pale tan blocky bodies penciled at the neck with black. They are peaceful in their dispositions and reassuringly chickenlike in their appearance.

The same could not be said for the Phoenix we also breed, of Japanese origin and sometimes called Yokohamas. Or at least not quite, for though the hens have a tight, elegant body, buff penciled with black, and the roosters are glossy red and black, like any southern dooryard mongrel cock, they have been bred for tails that can reach as long as fifteen feet. Such birds are of great value in Japan, classed as national treasures and never exported. Our oldest rooster is a poor shadow of them, with a tail only four feet long, but still he makes a noble and startling appearance. It is a peculiarity of the breed that they will seldom leave the perch to draggle their magnificent trains in the mud, one might think from pride, but actually because they have been bred over many centuries to stay aloft.

Of the smaller breeds, the tiny Old English gamecocks in red, black, white, blue, or banded "creele" (from the Old English word for a wicker basket); the equally small Modern Games, with upright bodies and long legs, causing them to look as if they walk on stilts; the Laced Rocks, elegantly penciled with white on a gray base; or the Cochins, self-assured white puffs of feather near to the ground, we breed only when our birds become old and we fear losing them. Most are never allowed to go broody, a condition into which hens fall when they have accumulated enough eggs to feel they are done with that business. Then their temperatures rise, their feathers fluff out, and they are content to fall into a sort of maternal dream for thirty days, leaving the nest only briefly to feed. The Cochins, however, are always allowed to brood, since they make superb foster mothers for other breeds. It is very easy to understand why, for nothing could seem more comfortable than their softly feathered bodies. Though each is hardly larger than a cantaloupe, they can accommodate twelve or even fifteen of the smaller eggs, and provide warm cuddling places for as many baby chicks, who peep out from beneath them, or sometimes even nestle in their feathered wings, with only alert little heads apparent. Baby chicks are born with all they need to survive except warmth, which artificially incubated birds know only in the form of a light bulb. But it seems far more pleasant—at least to us—to have a real mother; were we baby chicks ourselves, her feathered comfort and careful vigilance would be preferable by far to any light bulb. For this reason, though we mostly limit most breeds to two adult hens and a rooster, we keep six white Cochins, every one of which will be pressed into service as a foster mother at breeding time.

The baby guinea fowl, however, never get that maternal luxury. Though a Cochin would be quite content to set out a clutch of guinea eggs, not knowing the difference, baby guineas, from the second day of their lives, seem intent on winning some sort of marathon. They scatter wildly in search of food, and it is frustrating—if not impossible—for a placid Cochin to keep them all together. So they are artificially incubated, and raised in a heated brooder until they are old enough to be transferred to the flock. Even then all is not easy, for young birds (called keets) must be kept in the confinement of a pen until they are almost half grown, in order for them to learn their sense of place. Chickens will generally return to the safety of a poultry house to lay their eggs in nest boxes and to roost in safety at night. But guineas, though first raised by the Egyptians four thousand years ago, have never become completely domesticated. It simply does not lie within their nature. Though they belong, with chickens and turkeys, to the order Galliformes, they will prefer, if allowed to form the habit, to roost in trees, and will hide their nests in brushy thickets, where they may lay as many as twenty-five eggs. If setting goes well, the hen may reappear with almost as many small, gray athletic marbles, with which she is perfectly able to keep up, and in fact to lead on, in a mad dash across the countryside. But in the country at night, many creatures prowl silently—fisher cats, coyotes, feral dogs and cats, minks, raccoons, and weasles—always in search of a windfall such as a guinea hen on a large clutch of eggs will offer. Even should the eggs hatch, if it happens in the wild they will be shy of housing or of our presence, and many will go feral, not surviving their first harsh Vermont winter. So the guineas are trained carefully by a lengthy confinement as they grow up to roost in the rafters of the poultry house. And their eggs are taken for artificial incubation in early spring before they are released or their nests tracked down and robbed.

Interestingly enough, both this problem and its solution seem to have been known to the ancient Egyptians, who valued guineas for both their meat and eggs. They developed artificial incubators consisting of terra cotta tiles heated from beneath by decomposing camel manure, rather in the fashion of the old-fashioned hot-bed. Curiously, guineas appear not to have been kept either by the Greeks or Romans, though they knew of them. They reappeared in Europe only around the sixteenth century, when they were reintroduced by the Portuguese as a consequence of their exploration of the African coast.

Guineas are odd birds, both in their appearance and in their ways. Though their shape is familiar from depictions on ancient Egyptian frescoes and in African art, they are still startling-looking, almost prehistoric in their appearance. Their small, bony, naked heads terminate in a helmetlike peak, and seem far too insubstantial for their voluptuous bodies, domed across the back down to the tail. Their feet are frankly ugly, blotched irregularly with gray and yellow scales

and making surprisingly large tracks where they walk. Guineas have been bred to be completely white or buff, and many shades of lavender and even purple. But the original type, though common, is still very beautiful, a slate-gray ground spangled over with white dots, quite minute where they start below the neck but becoming progressively larger as they continue across the back and down the tail and wing feathers.

Another curious thing about guineas is their sound, or series of sounds. In the *Metamorphoses* Ovid identified guinea hens with the sisters of Meleager, whose mother, Althea, was told by the fates that Meleager's life would last only as long as the brand burning on the hearth at the hour of his birth endured. Cleverly, Althea extinguished and hid it. But when Meleager killed his uncles in a palace squabble, she angrily threw the brand into the fire, and the foretold result occurred. His sisters died of grief, but were retrieved by Artemis from Hades and turned into guinea hens. Still they continued to grieve, and their tears spangled their bodies. Presumably, also, they continued to shriek in woe.

When guineas are peaceful, they keep up a rather mournful, gentle, two-note sort of chatter among themselves. But at the approach of a stranger or any perceived menace, their chatter intensifies into a raucous screaming, one single note bursting rapid-fire from their throats with an ear-splitting, metallic sound. To most, it is as irritating as a shovel scraping against a buried rock; the sounds of all other barnyard animals can be imitated, but this cannot. Their vocal protests are useful, however, for they can frighten away predators and sound the alarm at any danger. For this reason if for no other, they are handy to have among the other poultry or simply about the place. One always knows when a hawk is soaring above, or an unexpected visitor pulls into the drive.

But of course the other reason for keeping guineas is for their meat. Though a young, dressed-out guinea is about the size of a small chicken, and may be prepared in many of the same ways, the resemblance stops there. The flesh of guineas is all dark meat, richly flavored, closer to pheasant in taste than to chicken. Because of their active, athletic habits, only young birds of eight months to a year old are useful for anything but stock. They are, however, a culinary treasure, for guineas are complete omnivores, and will, where allowed to do so, nourish themselves on a wide range of fruits, berries, grains, greens, and insects (including, to the gardener's joy, both slugs and Japanese beetles), all of which contribute flavor to their flesh. In the South, where they are more commonly kept than elsewhere, tender young birds are simply dredged in flour and fried, with no further thought to enhancement than perhaps a splash of pan milk gravy.

Even in the barnyard, guineas of the same age will vary in size, achieving as much as four pounds when dressed out, but more typically weighing in at around two pounds. For roasting, half a guinea per person should be figured. Because the breast meat, though flavorful, can tend to be dry, roast guinea must be basted frequently with butter in a little hot chicken stock, or possibly covered with strips of bacon. With that added richness of flavor, the dish seems to demand fairly strongly flavored side dishes, a puree of white beans perhaps, or tiny white turnips turned in oil and butter until they are tender and nut-brown. Homemade applesauce is nice too, our preference being the tartest of the four we make, from the fruit of the tree of 'Cox's Orange Pippin' growing at the back of the perennial garden. All this is for autumn, when rich flavors are best. But one must start planning

in the spring, when the eggs are laid, the tiny keets incubated and brooded, accustomed to their home, prepared for a destiny which is, to us at least, pleasant to contemplate.

If, with the return of light, there is a general preparation for spring among the birds in the poultry house and pigeon loft, the great forest trees among which we live also show signs of wakening. The definitive sign of spring's arrival in Vermont is the beginning of the sugaring season. As each day the temperature inches little by little toward a point above freezing, the sugar maples' sap begins to run. On any sunny day that reaches 40° or so, sap will drip even from broken buds and winter-damaged twigs. Then, up and down the roads and deep into the woods, all maple trees of any size will sport one bucket, and usually two or three. That, at least, is the old way, though more and more frequently one sees blue plastic tubing in place of the buckets, threading through the woods from tree to tree and draining eventually into a large galvanized-metal collecting tank.

From the point of view of passing tourists (and those people native Vermonters call "resident tourists"), the use of tubes represents the loss of considerable charm for the sake of efficiency. But then, the usual tourist has never had to carry heavy buckets full of sap through the woods, on a relentless schedule that does not admit of alteration even on bitter, blustery days; has never had a bucket of ice-cold sap spill into his boot, or found a whole family of drowned mice at the bottom. Those of us who make a gallon or two of syrup a year still use buckets, though even they are of the galvanized-metal kind, and never the beautiful old wooden ones, now mostly reserved for use as wastebaskets and planters for potted geraniums. Even farmers who earn a significant part of their yearly income from sugaring and

For the oldest living Vermonters, galvanized metal sap buckets are a utilitarian compromise, compared with the white-washed wooden buckets of the past. To us, however, they still carry an air of romance, in contrast to the ugly blue plastic tubing now generally in use. Still, perhaps all romance is underlain by hard work, and so these heavy buckets must be emptied twice a day when the sap runs well.

have converted to tubing must, however, also occasionally use buckets, to tap a tree that is isolated in a pasture or stands alone on a road. For thrift demands that every tree of appropriate size (which is to say, with a diameter equal to that of a bucket) should be tapped, no matter how inconveniently located it may be. Some of the very oldest trees are apt to be among them, occurring not in the "sugarbush" where trees grow in groves, but along roads and at the edges of mixed woods where a lack of competition has allowed them to attain ages of two hundred years or more. Some of these old trees, vast in bulk, will carry four or five buckets each season, as they have year after year for most of their long lives.

The sugaring season begins usually in early March, and lasts until the nights remain regularly above freezing. In a good year for sugaring—and a bad one for gardening—sap may remain of usable quality well into early April. During that period, twice a day if conditions are perfect, we empty buckets of sap into a large canning kettle and boil it down to its essence on the back of the stove. Maple syrup is precious—and expensive—because it takes so much sap and so much boiling time to produce it; thirty gallons of sap will reduce to slightly less than one gallon of syrup. When the sap is fresh from the tree, it is only mildly sweet, barely more than lightly flavored water. As it reduces, it gains flavor until it reaches syrup consistency, at which point, for home consumption, it is canned in pint glass jars. By then it will have achieved the deep amber color that most Vermonters prefer, and there is something curiously satisfying at this season to seeing the jars, in a gleaming row, lined up along the shelves.

Part of the satisfaction is of course the flavor of maple syrup, which has no substitute and which cannot be convincingly reproduced syn-thetically. ("Imitation maple flavor" is an oxymoron.) But another part is its connection with the past, as it forms a continuous link back to the first settlers, and to the Native Americans before them from whom they learned the art. In the Colonial period it was the only sweetening besides honey easily available. Called "Indian sugar," it was used in many foods, most notably baked beans, though most of what the early settlers ate seems to have been sweetened to some degree. (Maple syrup was still gladly put aside whenever brown sugar and molasses were available from the Caribbean, these being considered far more elegant.) There are still households in Vermont and in neighboring Quebec where it is the principal sweetener used, and there are old Vermonters who boast that they have never sat down to any meal—breakfast, dinner, or supper—without maple syrup in or on something. Even when other sweeteners are called for (as in Vermont pumpkin pie), maple syrup is considered obligatory as well.

But the love of maple syrup may be a regional or North American taste, for we have been told that most French people (except, to be sure, the Québecois) consider it unmitigatedly nasty. Perhaps they have never tried Vermont pumpkin pie. It might be made from canned pumpkin, but never is, a roasted four- or five-pound garden pumpkin of good flavor being the obligatory way to start. The flesh is spooned from the rind and pureed until it is smooth. To two cups of the puree, just about every spice on the shelf is added, but specifically, a teaspoon each of cinnamon and ginger, half a teaspoon of nutmeg, and a pinch each of clove and allspice, with half a teaspoon of salt. Two cups of heavy cream are then added (no compromises allowed), one fourth cup of dark rum, three large, lightly beaten fresh eggs, one cup (packed) of brown sugar, and the signature ingredient, a half cup of maple syrup. The whole is beaten together until smooth and satiny, and poured into an unbaked flaky pastry shell. Bake for about an hour in a moderate conventional oven heated to 350°, though the pie should be tested a little before (and possibly a little after) with a knife blade inserted in the center until it comes out clean. As all pumpkin pies seem to develop a crack square in the middle of the custard as they cool, it is a nice touch to fashion a maple leaf out of left-over pie crust, bake it separately, and place it, when the pie is cool, over this fault.

This recipe for pumpkin pie has taken us perhaps too rapidly from one of the greatest pleasures of early spring into the deep pleasure of autumn. We begin our syruping when the buds of the maples are tight-furled, hardly more than sharp, dull-green points along the bare stems. At that season, the seeds of pumpkins have not yet been sown, and even the varieties we will plant are still only things to fall asleep on, pondering. By the time the pumpkins have been selected and sown, the leaves of the maples will have hardened into the thick shade of summer. Throughout the hot, bright weather of July and August, the vines will grow, as wayward as vegetable guineas, studded here and there with great improbable lumps, redolent as they mature both of fairy tales and of the ancient heritage of our continent. When the maple leaves have turned transparent again, all into orange and tawny yellow, the pumpkins must be gathered to cure in the warmth of the house. As they lie in heaps and piles, their colors reflect the autumn garden, and are a fit emblem of the season. An emblem, too, is the pie they make, where beginning and end and all the processes in between are caught up in a perfect round. There is a deep delight in the idea, reminding us that life can be seamless, a contin-

uum that may still exist beneath the fracturing effects of modern life, a joining of start and finish. A pumpkin pie. One gardener in particular—an essential part of our town when we first came here to live (and garden) twenty years ago—first taught us that.

Our tiny village never had much of a downtown, and now it is shrunk to a one-room general store and a local pub. But in 1976 when we first came here, it was populous enough to seem, by contrast, positively teeming with life. There were two general stores, two places to buy gas and gossip, the pub that is here still (for the moment), and Jerry's Hardware. The original Jerry was actually named Girardo, Girardo Bolognani, and he was one of many who emigrated from Trentino–Alto Adijo in the Dolomites of northern Italy to this village early in the century. He had died some years before we came, but the business was carried on by his sons, Jim and Ernie, and it was one of the places everyone stopped on any routine trip to the village, not just for the odd bolt or pad of steel wool, but as much for the sustaining sense of life that was there, as lively and stimulating as the pub next door (which the Bolognani family also owned, and still does). It was a particularly important place for us, because we were building a house, and needed not only nails of an odd size and hinges and screening, paint thinner and paint and floor stain, but also—it seems now in embarrassing quantities—sound advice. Not just about building a house, but about gardening, for Jim, like almost everyone in the village then, was an avid gardener. So the gardening section of the hardware store was surprisingly well stocked, with seeds and fertilizers and sturdy tools, all very prominently displayed in the front of the store, just by the entrance. You could find out, if you lingered there for a minute, just what grapes would do well, just how to carry a potted orange or fig through a Vermont winter, but never (though we are sure it was done then, maybe still is) how to distill grappa of good quality from the surplus of fruit everyone had.

As a gardener, Jim Bolognani was by heritage and long experience among the best. But his practices were sometimes peculiar. He always started his tomatoes on Presidents' Day, a whole month at least before the books advised, or anyone else thought sensible. Pots of seed were covered with plastic film and stood in his basement, as close to the woodstove that heated the house as was possible. As soon as the seedlings appeared—very soon, in that humid and even warmth—he moved them down to the store to grow on in the bank of huge plate-glass windows that fronted the sidewalk and the street below. They were old windows, single thick panes that had never known storm sashes, though they were thickly caulked against drafts. Still, in early March, they dominated the coldest section of a distinctly cold store, which was heated only by another woodstove far in the back, where Jim's office was. The appearance of those tomato plants in the windows on Main Street was as sure a portent of spring's arrival as the new eggs in the henhouse or the running of the maple sap.

They were also a lesson in good gardening, as it had been done for over a century without much variation, and with results that perhaps can hardly be equaled by modern practice. Grown in very bright light but very cool temperatures, Jim's plants were the strongest we have ever seen, black-green, sturdy, and hard, with short bits of stem between the leaves, never drawn or attenuated or pale and fleshy. And when, near Memorial Day, we all set out our conventionally started plants in the garden, Jim's accepted the change in environment far more happily than others, and

required less covering, for having been kept cool all their lives. Nighttime lows in the forties—not unusual here in early summer—were no shock to them. They "caught" more quickly, grew more vigorously, and, best of all, bore crops ten days before anyone else's. The proof was by the cash register, on a plate.

Nothing like the ideal conditions of Jerry's Hardware obtains in most New England houses, or indeed, in home greenhouses, where they exist. Most of us must be content with the sunny windowsills we have, and so must delay the sowing of tomatoes until the light is higher in the sky and the days not so overcast. Less is lost by starting tomatoes a little later than by starting too early, for the wan little seedlings will reach for whatever illumination they can get, but their pale and watery complexions will cause them to look like children who have watched too much television. Unlike almost any other vegetable seedling, they can be planted deep, the stretched nodes buried in a hole with only the growing tip exposed. The shock of real outdoor light will be great, however, and some shading—until they "catch"—will be required. It is far better to start seeds later, and the usual recommendation is to seed eight weeks before the first frost-free date (June 1 for us). Crops will be delayed a week or two, but in a good year they will still be heavy.

But celery and, more important to us, celeriac are less forgiving. Both germinate slowly, and grow slower, at least at first, so a later sowing, anything much after early March, may result in not just a later crop but little crop at all. Celery stems will be so small and stringy that they will be good for hardly anything but soup stocks, and celeriac will form such little knobs of root that they will not be worth the laborious peeling. Celery is common enough, and good started plants may be bought from garden centers at the

❧ *Though infant tomato plants have hardly sprouted from the seed, it is good to put their supports in place in early spring, before the great press of other chores begins. Eight-foot bamboo poles are lashed together into a frame beautiful in itself, each frame supporting one antique tomato variety.*

appropriate planting time; failing that, though there is no replacement for a crop one has grown oneself, celery of good quality is always available in markets at a modest price. But started celeriac plants are rare even in good nurseries, and the ideal end result of its culture, a knobby root the size of a grapefruit, ivory white through and through, can be found usually only in the finest gourmet grocery stores, and only at the finest gourmet prices. Both crops are very important to us, first because of the growing conditions they relish. Whereas most vegetable crops require well-drained soil and as much sun as they can get, the celeries relish damp, mucky soil and some light afternoon shade, just the conditions that obtain in a far corner of our vegetable garden near the poultry house. Both crops keep very well through the winter, though according to different methods. In autumn, celery is dug with its root system entire, packed upright in wooden apple crates with a little soil about the roots, watered in, and stood in a cool storage shed with only a little illumination—a single bright light bulb will do—positioned over it to keep the leaves and stems from turning ghostly white and flavorless. Celeriac is lifted also before frosts touch it, but the straggling roots and tops are cut away from the knob, never so close as to wound its skin. The knobs (clinging dirt and all, for that helps them keep) are then put in plastic bags and stored in the bottom of an old refrigerator turned to its lowest setting. (The upper shelves are handy for chilling spring bulbs for forcing.) Stored this way, celery will keep at least to Christmas, and celeriac almost to spring, or for as long as it lasts. But neither will be worth the storage unless they have been seeded very early, grown on under the best conditions one has, planted out while at the peak of their youthful vigor, and given a long season to mature. For

years, therefore, they occupied all the cool, sunny windowsills we had.

And tomatoes, which we sowed two or three weeks later, were not their only competitors for space. In that magical time frame that most garden books (not in Jim Bolognani's) describe as "eight to twelve weeks before the last frost-free date in your area" came—in quick succession—peppers, eggplants, broccoli, cabbage, cauliflower, Brussels sprouts, onions, leeks, radicchios, and more and more annuals, of rare or select varieties, grown to ornament the summer flower garden. For a New England house, ours is unusually blessed with windows, and they are unusually (our neighbors would say unthriftily) large. Nor are we averse to stumbling over flats of seedlings on our way to the piano or the telephone, or to shifting about pots of needful seedlings as the light shifts from window to window. But the most we had—both of windows and of patience—was not enough, and so we reluctantly turned to fluorescent grow-lights in the basement. The late Katherine White once tartly said (in her wonderful book *Onward and Upward in the Garden*) that she was prepared to be a floor nurse, but not an electrician. We felt somewhat the same, but the results of growing plants under lights, eerie as the glow of them was, surprised us. Seedlings were strong and short, rich with healthy leaves, and it was comforting to think of all that life down there, growing away in what had been before a rather dark and dusty spot. But our list of plants to seed grew faster, comprising thirty sorts of tomato, twenty of pepper, ten of eggplant, each one of a different variety, artichokes, cardoons, more and more forms of radicchio, more annuals, more tender vines. We needed only a plant or two from each separate seeding, but we found it almost impossible to discard the rest, so healthy were they, and the excess so desirable, to someone else.

Providentially, just as we began to feel that we had reached—or actually exceeded—our capacity for starting our own seed, we met Jack Manix and his wife, Karen. They are the heirs to Walker Farm in Dummerston, Vermont, one of the state's original eighteenth-century farmsteads, a property that has remained in Jack's family for eight generations—indeed, has never been owned by any other. They were determined to wrest a living from the land, though they knew that could probably not be done by dairy farming, even though their sixty acres of bottomland lying along the Connecticut River was some of the richest in the state. They turned instead to raising vegetables for local residents in Brattleboro and other nearby towns, and opened a roadside stand that attracted a growing number of summer visitors. Soon their customers began asking for started plants of vegetables and flowers. One plastic tube house was built, and rapidly multiplied into others. (Jack became adept at growing tomatoes in the ground within one, hand-polinating them, and then removing the plastic when the weather settled, thus offering organically grown, vine-ripened Vermont tomatoes by late June.) Both Jack and Karen were eager to expand their offerings, and we were eager to find someone who would deal carefully and lovingly with seed we had culled from foreign catalogs and obscure American ones, collected on trips and dried in Kleenex that should have been reserved for runny noses, or had been given by other gardeners. So we were all a perfect match.

We should hasten to say, however, that Jack and Karen have long since outrun us in their pursuit of rare and heirloom vegetables, new and unusual annuals, container plants, and tender perennials. At the peak of the planting season in early June, their stand (nursery, one should now say) boasts a dazzling selection of herbs, annual and tender plants, and, best of all, heirloom and obscure vegetables. We have quit worrying whether we should order seed of tomatoes such as 'Mortgage Lifter' or 'Pruden's Purple' or 'Yellow Pear,' of vines such as 'Cobaea scandens' or 'Mina lobata,' or annuals such as 'Ammi majus' or the stately castor beans. They are sure to be there. Certainly there are gardeners who consider relying on someone else to start their seeds tantamount to giving up their children to be nursed by another breast, but we are not among them. It is a huge luxury to have strong seedlings ready when it is time to plant them and one is able to do it, and an even greater one to acquire really rare seed knowing that it will be grown well, thus preserving its rarity and making it accessible to others. There is a clear symbiotic relationship between good gardeners and good garden centers, though one has to feel, surveying the general offerings in most garden centers, that it could work better than it does, that it could work as well as ours does with Walker Farm. It is a system, perhaps, that people should think of tampering with.

Unlike Jack Manix, we are neither of us children of the country, though we have taken to its ways with a vengeance, and it now seems to us that we could have lived the bulk of our life in no other way. Still, the decisions of youth are relatively arbitrary, and could easily have gone otherwise. We might by now, for example, have dominated the complexities of New York, known its obscurer neighborhoods, mastered the contents of its rich museums, or at least, their floor plans. That, as it happens, would have been something also to possess. But as it turned out, we submerged ourselves instead in country life, and resolved to draw from it all that might be offered. Like so many of our generation who made that decision, we set out initially to grow as much of our own food as we practically could.

Lacking an ample inheritance or any other unearned source of income, what that meant in practical terms was that we would tend a large flower garden, our first love, and its edible counterpart, while also earning our living, first as teachers, then as garden designers, and later as garden writers. To these considerable burdens on our time we added the conviction that since the strictest vegetarianism did not seem to suit us, we would grow our own meat as well. We started with creatures that were relatively easy to raise—pigeons, ducks, geese, and chickens—which supplied us both with eggs and with meat. We soon graduated to lambs and sheep, and to an occasional pig, so amiable always that we thought we could never part with it, until its growing bulk and determined ways made us glad, at the end, to see it as packages of neatly wrapped "cuts" in the freezer. We got a brief lesson from goats, so willful and demanding that we have never repeated the experiment. And finally, we acquired cows.

With us, aesthetics have always run an uneasy race with practicality, and so the breed we chose, Scots Highlands, were selected as much for their great, shaggy bodies and impressive horns as for any thought of the table. But as cows go, they are remarkably self-sufficient. They are sturdy and winter-proof, far preferring shelter in the woods to a barn, a good thing for us as we had no barn, and certainly not the time to clean it. They are also omnivorous grazers, as happy with brush and blackberry bushes as with pasture grass, and our deep, mature woods grew much more of the former than the latter. They have kept the woodland clean, so that the great boles of maple and beech, the odd oak and scattering of winter-black hemlock, rise from a close-clipped floor, as it is nicest that they should. In the main, also, they are tractable beasts, easily confined by electric fencing and docile, so long as one does not ask them to vary their accustomed patterns of hoof, or do anything that seems strange and new to them. They live for twenty years, on the average, and when they die, it is quite sudden and quick, leaving us with the only problem they have ever created here, which is what, exactly, to do with a fifteen hundred–pound corpse. Best of all, they bear their young without fuss, and rear them well, asking—indeed insisting on—no tampering from us. With one exception.

In our herd of six, consisting of a vast bull named Titus and five cows, there is one, Livia, that we chose for her special beauty, for though the rest are shades of red typical of the breed, she is milk-white, and unusually elegant. She has, however, a physiological problem not unusual in cows bred for meat rather than predominantly for milking. After her first successful calving, a magnificent little snow-white bull, her teats never again regained their muscle tone, but remained distended to such an extent that the next calf could not get his nursing mouth around them, and almost died of starvation before we discovered the problem. Short of allowing her annual calf to die, there is no solution but to take it from her, just in the first hours of birth before she has bonded with it or indeed even understands what has happened. So, sometime in the first week of April, like clockwork, she gives birth and we steel ourselves to enter the pasture, hook the calf from beneath her with an old walking cane kept ready, bundle its slimy and surprisingly heavy newborn body in our arms, and run like hell for the house. She mourns only a little, more we think from the discomfort of the milk distending her udder than from any sense of loss. And as she is annually spared the burdens of nursing throughout the spring and summer, she is extraordinarily healthy, even for a cow, and bears magnificent calves.

❡ *Though weeds begin to become abundant by the end of early spring, good pasturage is scarce, and so the cows must still be fed their winter hay. But they richly return what they are given, in the form of compost and manure, both the envy of cowless gardeners everywhere. Julia, visibly pregnant and soon to give birth, claims an extra ration for herself.*

It is far easier to comfort Livia, however, than the calf. An extra bucket of grain seems to do it for her. But the calf, brand-new to the world, has pressing needs, for warmth, for a good scrub all over with a dry towel (as much as it will ever know of a mother's rasping tongue), and for colostrum, the first milk that descends after birth, as rich and thick and yellow as an egg custard. Without a pint or so of that, the calf will never acquire a healthy immune system, or develop into a thrifty animal. And so, around mid-March (just to be on the safe side) we call the Wheelers. Like the Manixes, they are an old family in our valley who have occupied their land for generations and have always maintained a thrifty dairy herd. From year to year it is our only annual contact

with them, though years ago we taught several of the Wheeler children, and the goodwill appears to be there. Mrs. Wheeler is never surprised by our call, simply saying, "About that time of year, I guess. Thought you'd call soon. We have a birth coming in a day or so. I'll put some by." And so, in a day or two, we stop at the Wheeler farm, to be handed a gallon-sized plastic ice-cream carton, full of the substance that will be required. It goes into the freezer, where it may stay until we defrost and warm it for our calf's first meal.

What follows then is one of the most exacting, and most satisfying, duties of early spring. Three times a day the calf must be nursed from a giant, quart-sized baby bottle. As it develops, its demand for more milk becomes fierce, and so someone must make a milk run on a regular basis to the Corse Farm, another of those settled old enterprises (in the hands of the same family since 1860) that are the strength of our rural community. It specializes in extraordinarily rich, cream-laden milk from fat Jersey cows, and the five-gallon plastic bucket, when it is picked up, is often still warm. In the beginning, five gallons will last three days, later two, and then only a day. To pay for it, we leave an envelope in the milk room, with the requisite amount in small change hoarded from the bottoms of our pockets through the year, literally milk money, atop the empty bucket. We could, of course, save ourselves that bother (and some of the expense) by using soy-based milk substitute, which comes dry in fifty-pound bags, but which is laced with hormones and antibiotics. It seems best to nourish our calf on nature's own product, and we have never had one that was less than perfectly healthy and magnificently thrifty in its growth.

While that growth lasts. And that is (to hasten the end of this tale) about twelve or fourteen weeks. Then the calf is shot, as quickly and painlessly as possible, and the carcass delivered to another neighbor, another Trentino émigré named Mario Christofolini, who is retired now but who still butchers occasionally for friends, with a skill that amounts to consummate art. The end result is veal of a quality that cannot be bought anywhere in this country, the consequence of uncompromising care in raising and,

❧ *Because of a genetic deformity, which makes her unable to nurse, sad, rakish Livia has managed to keep only one of her babies, and that only because we played the role of a second mother, standing beside her with a giant baby bottle in hand. Since then, all her offspring have been stolen from her shortly after their births, and nursed by us in a quiet, warm stall.*

By the end of early spring, the first sowing and planting of hardy crops may begin. Members of the large onion clan are among the hardiest, and so seedling leeks may be lined out as early as the soil can be worked. They are peculiarly satisfying to plant, since after an hour or two, something green and promising will exist where before was only bare, waiting earth.

from the calf's point-of-view, a life that, while short, has been perfectly sweet. We make no apology for our veal.

The burdens of early spring are not perhaps greater than the burdens of any other season, but they tend to be more exacting. Poultry must be divided up for breeding, increasing the number of food and water bowls that must be filled each day. Eggs must be safely accumulated in a cool place for hatching, turned twice daily as the hen would in her nest, until a Cochin obliges by going broody and taking charge of things herself. Sap buckets must be emptied twice a day, for as long as the sap runs, and the sugaring kettle must be watched carefully, lest a whole batch scorch and be spoiled. Seed must be selected, ordered from a dozen or more catalogs, and delivered to Jack and Karen Manix for germina-tion at the proper time. Mrs. Wheeler must be called for colostrum. Livia has to be observed carefully, day and evening and sometimes, when we sense her time is very near, in the night. Once the calf is born, the milk runs must begin, and milk must be heated and the bottle offered three times a day. All these things must occur in the midst of lives that do seem to have gotten more complicated in other ways. But it has always been true of both of us that once we have loved doing something, it is an extreme situation that will cause us to think of not doing it. Preserved in the rituals of early spring are all the enthusi-asm of our youthful selves, and so far—for the moment still—we have not been required to turn loose much that we have loved. In the exhaustion that characterizes this season, and the one next to come, there is great comfort in that.

High Spring

For the nongardening world, and even for gardeners who are less compulsive than we, less driven or greedy, there is magic in the very words "high spring." Slowly, tentatively, temperatures begin warming in late March, the "lamb" part of that otherwise dreadful month, and by April, copious rains and progressively milder days and nights unlock the earth. In New England it is a slow waking—as all waking should be—a gentle and gradual shift from the sleep of deep winter to the full, bright morning of early summer, with pleasant yawns and stretches, dozings and wakings, an easy falling back and forth between two states, a mild transition. That is, at any rate, the ideal, and we must envy people who experience the arrival of spring in that way.

But it seems true of us that no transition is ever easy, that all endings and beginnings, and the states in between, require deep breaths, a tensening of soul and sinew, a girding of the loins.

Though the tasks of winter are physically demanding, winter asks little of us except to surrender to its soft and steady rhythms, its deep sleep. In that it is like high summer, or autumn, where each task occupies its own space without much reference to all else that must be done. Pleasure in the doing of one single thing, shoveling snow or hauling wood or tending the animals, is not crowded out by the anxiety of other things that must be done, soon, now, even while one works at something else. In the settled seasons of the year, one never wants to be two people, fragmented not to double pleasure, but just to get things done. But in high spring, parts of oneself seem to go off in different directions. It is not a pleasant sensation, and sometimes it seems like the dislocation of a mild illness—a bad cold or the flu—that only the passage of time can cure.

All that is not of course to say that high spring does not bring pleasures. By mid-May, the garden, and especially the lane up to the vegetable garden, is rich with daffodils, hundreds planted in large drifts of individual forms. The old beech and maple woods that embrace the meadow are waves of blue, from an original planting of fifteen thousand chionodoxa, now happily multiplying in the deep wood loam to thousands more. If late frosts let them, deciduous magnolias, chiefly the small, muscular *Magnolia stellata* and its taller children from matings with *M. kobus* will spangle their gray branches thickly with stars of white for two weeks or more. When they fade, apples and crab apples take their place, flowering so richly that they are clouds of white or pale pink settled on the garden. Tulips become abundant, first the delicate species ones and then the taller Darwin types, and there are many flowering shrubs—quinces and forsythias, weigelas, rhododendrons, and deciduous azaleas. *Vinca minor,* our most faithful ground cover, lightens its reliable, dark-green carpet with delicate blue periwinkle stars, and, in rarer varieties, with flesh pink or icy white. It is a good time to float through the garden, simply enjoying the wealth that is there, all suddenly, and the wealth of things to come.

But in fact, the flowers of late spring are all warnings, alarm bells actually, for labor that is to be done. Old gardeners lived not so much by the calendar, since weathers, from year to year, are so variable, as by the signs of nature, and chiefly by the wisdom of flowering shrubs and trees, which open in some years a week earlier, in others two weeks later. So, though spinach and radishes and broad beans might be planted "as soon as the frost is out of the ground," other crops must wait for less ambiguous signs. Potatoes and peas are best planted when the forsythia flowers, and lettuces and other salad crops do best when seeded then as well. The great planting of the vegetable garden, with beans and corn, carrots, celeries, broccoli, cabbages, cauliflower, Brussels sprouts, all the other coles and onions, had best wait until the apple blossoms fall. And the true tropicals—cucumbers, peppers, tomatoes, eggplants, squashes, and pumpkins—should wait for seeding or transplanting until the peonies are fat in bud. Even before all that, however, there is much to do, so much, in fact, that the daffodils go by in a blur, and the chionodoxa is only a blue haze, glimpsed over our shoulders as we tote bags of lime up to the garden.

It is always our hope that much of the work of preparing the vegetable garden for spring sowing will have been done in autumn, when days are brisk, energy is high, and muscles have been put into discipline by a long summer of outdoor labor. As late crops are gathered, tomato vines stripped of their partially ripe and green fruit, pumpkins and winter squash trundled down in wheelbarrows, ripe pods of beans stripped away for drying and the haulms thrown to the chickens, then or shortly after, in the two or three weeks of fine, clear weather that is early autumn, then is the time to clear the garden of late, lurking weeds, bring in buckets of cow muck, toss the rows high to expose as much ground surface as possible to winter, and generally, to restore to the vegetable garden its skeletal beauty. When the work is done then, as it should be, there is beauty enough in the sculpted earth; and come spring, the labor is easy. We are required only to rake down the rows to the fine tilth that only good autumn preparation can give, and put in the first early seed. But it is not only the wisdom of good culture, or the satisfaction of seeing everything trim and tidy for winter that recommend the work of putting the vegetable garden to rights in autumn. Come spring—come high spring—there will be so much else to be done that spongy, winter-soft muscles and a spirit wakened too suddenly to so many other chores will not be equal to the labor. It is a great comfort, then, to have the vegetable garden already in good shape after its long winter rest.

When autumn's work has been done well, the vegetable garden sits as an oasis of order and control in the seething chaos of so many other tasks. So, in all the press of springtime work— the pruning, feeding, weeding, and planting that call out from every other corner of the garden— it is no burden to retreat there. Rather, it is a positive relief. The sowing of the first season's crops is gentle, reflective work, largely unhampered by the stress of getting things right and ready for the even spacing of radish seeds, the sprinkling in of lettuce and mesclun, the neat regimentation of onion sets, lined out from their paper bag and gently eased into the ripe earth.

There may even be, at day's end, an early crop to bring back to the kitchen, in a basket emptied of its burden of seeds and sets. There are only a few vegetables that will live over the winter in our cold garden. Perhaps the choicest is asparagus, and for its early greenness, tasting of health, we keep a large old bed, faithfully over-composted and limed in autumn for the promise of young shoots in May. In April they are only promise, though something in its way as fine needs only two weeks past the final melting of the snow to be ready for the table. Egyptian or "tree" onions have been a part of our garden as long as we have gardened together. We found them naturalized along the Fenway in Boston, and transplanted them into our first little allotment garden there, now thirty years ago. We have carried the stock through several gardens in rented houses in Massachusetts and Vermont, and once we settled here, they were moved about the property from one tentative vegetable garden to the next, until they found a home as permanent as our own life here will be, in the split-rail confines we distinguish from its predecessors as *the* vegetable garden.

Egyptian onions are curious plants, once treasured in Colonial gardens for their capacity to fill "the hungry gap" between the last winter storage crops and the first wild gatherings with something green and full of vitamins. Now, however, they are largely grown as curiosities, with little sense of their rich and ancient culinary possibilities. Among the hardiest of all perennial onions, they are pure ease to grow, forming thick clumps with very little in the way of fertilizer or soil amendments and even naturalizing in abandoned pastures or, as we first found them, along the Fenway. The clumps come green very early in the spring, some two weeks or better before the first wild dandelions may be harvested from the

High Spring

In the great press of high-spring chores, it is always a wonderful thing if the garden has been cleared in autumn of last season's crops, composted, and left to mellow through the winter. Then it is as stimulating to a gardener as a clean, prepared canvas is to a painter. Here, lima beans are being transplanted from seed sown in peat pots, as they relish a cool but frost-free spring.

❧ *Egyptian, or "tree," onions are winter-hardy well into zone 4, and become usable early in March, thus being the first crop we harvest from the garden and, raw or cooked, the first spring treat. All that remains now is a solitary, lusty clump to provide sets for next year's crop, though a few tender leaves might still be stolen to season an omelette.*

lawn. At that stage, each separate shoot is coated in the slimy remains of last year's growth, but that is easily stripped away to reveal a fresh green shoot. They are excellent as raw scallions, or when trimmed into uniform neatness they may be lightly browned on each side in a skillet with a little butter to make "poor man's asparagus." From this stage, they may be given a further, more elaborate treatment by coating them with a light cream sauce, dusting them with hard Italian cheese and bread crumbs, and sending them under the broiler for a wonderful gratin.

The scallion season for Egyptian onions is brief, hardly more than a month, from mid-March to mid-April in Vermont, after which they become tough and rank. But unless one has been too greedy, more goodness will come. Each mature plant will send up one or more thick, tubular stems surmounted by a giddy arrangement of tiny bulbils, which may be pickled for cocktail onions or pounded with a pestle for a taste like garlic. Even the mature leaves and young, hollow stems can be used, if one wishes, by piping them full of softened cream cheese with a cake decorator, chilling them, and slicing them into neat rounds to top canapés. Thus, as with so many members of the onion clan, silk purses may be made from sow's ears.

The management of Egyptian onions in the garden is very simple. Indeed, in most gardens, they are not managed at all, but rather left to flourish in an odd, weedy corner, where they may be harvested in season, or not. We try to have no such corners in our garden, and so, when the heads of bulbils are ripe in autumn, we harvest them from what is left of the previous crop, and replant them in a fresh row. The old plants are then discarded, and the original row prepared for some other crop. Autumn-sown bulbils will produce good spring scallions and leaves, stems, and

tops for midsummer use, and three or four clumps left in place at the end of the row will supply enough bulbils to resow for the following year. With such management, once one has a stock of Egyptian onions, one need never beg or buy it again.

So it is also with other "scallion" types of onions, grown not for their enlarged bulbs but for their edible shoots and tops. The word "scallion" is a huge confusion among those who raise onions, however, since any onion can be harvested (from direct seeding, from transplants, or from "sets," small, dry, immature onions) as soon as there is enough crunch in them to be tempting. Indeed, it is usual to plant bulbing onions rather thickly and harvest every other one as thinnings to be enjoyed as green onions and make room for larger bulbs to develop. But true scallions are a different race from bulbing onions, in that their bases will never enlarge beyond a certain, skinny degree; rather, they will continue to divide and divide, making thick clumps in the manner of a close relative, culinary chives. Among this group, several are winter-hardy well into zone 4, and can be treated like any other hardy perennial and divided year after year for steady increase.

Among true scallions the standard is 'Beltsville Bunching,' which is probably the "multiplier onion" one might remember from the garden of one's grandparents. Putting that sentiment aside, 'Beltsville Bunching' has serious rivals in the Japanese 'Ho Shi Ko' and its varieties, and one of them is what we think we grow in our vegetable garden for midspring harvest as green onions. We "think" so, because our source was no more elevated than a bin of the local supermarket, where tidy bunches were on display, each with enough basal tissue and new root to suggest that they might be planted out, as an experiment. They could have been simply immature bulbing onions, but in fact they settled down to "bunch" and to become perennial, and the results have closely resembled catalog descriptions of 'Ho Shi Ko.' With 'Beltsville Bunching,' they nicely bridge the gap between the last Egyptian onions and the first thinnings of globing onions planted from seed or sets.

Such experiments, when they are successful, also endear plants to gardeners. So we treasure our supermarket variety, whatever it may actually be, though we know that the most superior scallions are bred from other Japanese cultivars that are not truly hardy, at least in Vermont, and so must be started anew early each spring from seed. Among the best is 'Ishikura,' which may be mounded with earth or blanched in the more decorative Japanese fashion with clay drainage tiles to form foot-long snow-white scallions. 'Tokyo Long' is grown more for its rigid, arrow-straight green tops than for its whitened base, and it would be the one to use if one were given to tying bundles of vegetables into artful packages with green "ribbon." 'Red Beard,' though somewhat stumpy, with a fanned green top, has nether parts as scarlet as rhubarb. We have grown all these, but we prefer our reliably perennial types, which we greet with fresh pleasure as old friends when they return each spring, and which we divide and repropagate, thus stitching the years together.

But if high spring is the season for harvesting green onions, it is also the time to plant bulbing onions, from seedlings or sets, for an autumn harvest. It is certainly true that onions of decent quality can almost always be had from the supermarket. Generally they are classified according to no more sophisticated a system than their color—red for hamburgers and salads; white for boiling, creaming, and pickling; and yellow for most any purpose, but particularly for slow-simmered sauces, stews, and soups. Beyond these distinctions, most cooks worry little about their choice of onions, for onions are not generally like other vegetables—corn or peas, asparagus or artichokes—which are at their best when harvested fresh and prepared within minutes of picking. Rather, onions are staples, like flour or sugar or salt, one of those things that are simply kept on hand. Modern breeders have aimed their efforts at creating bulbing onions that remain firm and sprout reluctantly in storage, and that are also quite pretty, with shiny skins and a heft as irresistible as a baseball. So for most people, an onion is just an onion, responsible in itself for no more finesse than to be uniform in quality, fairly versatile in use, and within the margin of pungency that is considered tolerable.

Given these truths, some wonder how cultivating onions in the home garden can be worth the trouble. As committed vegetable gardeners, we often confront this question, and our answer—never logical, certainly never "price-conscious"—always comes down (as do most such challenges about one's life) to one unchallengeable answer: "Because . . . because it gives us *pleasure* to do it." And the pleasures we find in cultivating onions are in fact considerable. To begin with, for us, gardening (like its allied art, cooking) is one of the best ways one has to connect with the past. In each spring's sowings of onion seeds or planting of sets, we know that we are cultivating one of the crops most anciently associated with humanity. Earliest

❧ RIGHT: *Almost any member of the onion clan, including shallots, leeks, garlic, and bulbing onions, may be eaten with relish in the green, immature stage. So, as with this row of shallots, we plant thickly, planning to harvest every other one from high spring to early summer as "green onions."*

records concerning onions have to do with religion, food, and death; as the three are hardly separable, onions appear prominently, showing up in the most ancient market tallies, in accounts of the daily rations supplied workers on the great pyramids, and as a cult of worship in Egypt, where the onion was accorded divine honors. One could buy a roasted onion from street vendors in the Chaldean city of Ur, and it is pleasant to us to suppose that it would not have tasted much different from a yellow-skinned 'Stuttgarter' we harvest in autumn from spring-planted sets and cook to a caramelized gold in parchment for an autumn feast.

With each onion set we plant, and each onion we harvest in late summer, we recognize the beauty of the typical form, a slightly flattened globe with a gracefully tapering top. We are hardly the first, for that shape has become the architectural signature both of the mosques of Islam and of Eastern Rite churches. Even the word "onion" is beautiful, deriving through medieval French from the Latin *unio,* signifying oneness and integrity (and, except for the last consonant, identical to our word "union"). Onions figure in every cuisine of the world. They were the first gifts made by Columbus to the New World in recompense for the many he took away. (Initially, they did not thrive here.) Many cultures have recognized in the onion life-giving and therapeutic properties, a belief that has now migrated from folk wisdom firmly into medical science. Finally, the prominence of the onion in human experience has been celebrated in many proverbs and sayings, as in the French "*Occupe-toi de tes oignons,*" which translates bluntly into "Mind your own business." "Onion tears" are a designation of insincerity in English for obvious reasons, and in both England and France, folk wisdom has it that the thickness of the "leaves" of an onion bulb indicates the severity of the winter to come.

All that human history and lore inheres in any onion we plant or harvest, reminding us that gardening, and vegetable gardening particularly, connects us to all that has gone before in the struggles of our race to survive, welds our own brief years one to another (whether in struggle or pleasure or both) and—in the arts we master, the knowledge we pass on, and, quite simply, in the way we spend our days—provides a repository (at best, of wisdom and beauty, at worst, of diverting amusement) to those who must come after. All that is rather a grand answer to the question of why we plant so many onions each spring. But it is in our minds as we do it, causing us to think that the simple onion is in itself a synecdoche of all the answers one might give to the question of why one raises vegetables at all.

Each year, when barrels full of shiny onion sets first appear in the local Agway, so full of life and so polished and complete in themselves, we find we can't resist buying a scoop or two of brown, white, and red. But one onion we grow can never be found there, and must be raised from seed sown in early spring. That is the old Italian variety called cipollini, or "button onion," so-called because the mature bulb is flattened into a disk little more than an inch thick. Those grown in our garden have a lovely, sweet flavor, not perhaps as gentle as Vidalias (which we cannot grow, because they require short summer days, and ours are long), but close enough to cause us to prize them. They are also

❧ RIGHT: *Shallots, though inordinately expensive in markets, are easy to grow in cool gardens. Sown early in spring, they produce abundant autumn crops, most of which will be braided for winter use. A few, however, the smallest, are pushed back into the ground for spring scallions, or to develop into the next autumn's crop.*

great keepers, especially if woven into ropes and hung high in the coldest part of the kitchen or the dry cool of the cellar stairs. Of course, we are not harvesting cipollinis in April, but rather, only transplanting the frail green hairs of tiny seedlings into rows in winter-mellowed soil. It is tedious work, and they seem so fragile that one wonders whether they will catch and thrive to produce a crop by late summer and early autumn. They always do, for onions—life-giving as they have always been assumed to be—are also surprisingly tenacious of life, and are among the easiest of all garden crops to grow.

Not all we sow in these first days of true spring require an entire summer to mature, as bulbing onions do. Many spring crops are quick to reach edible size, and so are satisfying both in themselves and for the prompt returns they make. Perhaps the quickest are the radishes, most forming good-sized globes in fewer than thirty days from seed. And though they alone could hardly make a meal in themselves, their presence on the table in May is a gustatory pleasure equal in its fashion to corn or fresh peas. For never, in season or out, can one buy a radish that tastes even remotely like one just pulled from the ground. There is an earthy mineral freshness that comes from a real radish grown in one's own garden soil and eaten within minutes of harvest. For the gardener, there is also something tremendously optimistic about a radish. It is not only that when they thrive to perfection they indicate a soil capable later, when they are cleared away, of supporting more substantial crops, beans, tomatoes, or corn. The way they leap into life, germinating in two or three days from their fat seed and progressing from sturdy seedling to delicious youth in only three or four weeks, reassures us after winter's sleep that there is life in the world— quick, lusty, generous, and promising.

All radishes are grouped under the botanical name *Raphanus sativus,* but they are so anciently associated with humanity that no certain wild progenitor exists. Closest is the weedy charlock, *R. raphanistrum,* which exists throughout the Mediterranean and in the early nineteenth century, we are told, still flourished picturesquely in the decayed stone of the Collosseum at Rome. Whether it was in fact a native species or came there in ancient times with the fodder imported for the wild beasts kept there, none can say, though of course the latter possibility is the more interesting to ponder. Ancient records do verify, however, that garden radishes migrated from northern China to India, and thence to the Mediterranean as a result of trade. Thus, any radish seed one shakes out of the packet and into one's hand for spring planting has within it a history of thousands of years of cultivation and selection, and owes its very existence not to Nature but to the agency of man.

Garden radishes exist in two classifications. The first is quick of growth, and is sown as early as the ground may be worked in spring for late-spring and early-summer consumption. With hot weather, radishes in this class become rank and woody, but where late summers are cool and moist, as are ours in Vermont, an additional sowing is made in mid-August for an autumn crop. Within this group our favorite is the cultivar called 'French Breakfast,' not only because we like the name and the idea, but also because its long, narrow roots are beautiful, bright red with a white base, and its flavor is at once sweet and pungent, never merely crunchy water. 'Cherry Belle' is faithful and pretty, with its uniform red globes and neat, leafy tops; and 'Easter Egg' is amusing, with globes in many shades of deep and pale red, purple, and white. All these are old standbys, easily available from almost any seed company, though each year's offerings include new varieties, tempting either for their name or form, or both. The best flavor in a radish, however, seems to us to depend more on weather, culture, and the time of harvest than on the specific claims of individual varieties. Of these three variables, timing seems the most important—though the weather must be cool and the soil friable and rich with minerals (though not so much with nitrogen, which makes rank growth and a woody root). For a radish of this early sort is really only in prime condition for two or three days, and radishes have an uncanny way of sneaking up on, and passing by, the eager harvester. So in late spring we check the rows daily as we go about our other tasks. Many are eaten in the garden, after just a brush across our jeans, for a little dirt on a fine radish is not such a terrible thing. The rest come down to the kitchen, to fill bowls small or large according to the day's yield. Washed and sitting on the table next to a little old Japanese bowl full of salt that is always there, they rarely make it to a meal, even breakfast. They are a fine but transitory pleasure, too transitory unless one has taken care to sequester one's full share.

The second group of radishes, called *Raphanus sativus* var. *longipinnatus* by botanists and by culinary experts of a botanical slant, are both treated differently in the garden and in the kitchen, and seem, in both their behavior and their culinary uses, much more closely allied to turnips than to radishes. They were a staple of the European table from the Middle Ages to the eighteenth century, and were a sturdy, reliable vegetable for American cooks until the early nineteenth century. Most certainly, some form of this radish was what the English diarist Samuel Pepys records having eaten, hot and buttered, at the house of William Penn. Except for the wonderfully continuous thread of American gardeners that saved and sowed their own seed, however, this group of radishes dropped largely out of the repertory of American cooking, to the extent that Fannie Farmer, in the first edition of her *Boston Cooking School Cookbook* (1896) could firmly state, "Radishes are used merely for a relish, and are served uncooked."

Today, however, there is a renewed interest in radishes of the *longipinnatus* group, encouraged on the one hand by culinary historians and creative restaurateurs, bent on recovering experience of those foods our ancestors either relished or depended on (or hopefully both) and on the other by the modern cook's interest in the reintroduction of anything good that was once enjoyed and might be again. Asian cooking, too, has contributed powerfully to this interest, treasuring as it does many varieties of the group, such as daikon or the fabled Chinese 'rose' radish, with coral-pink flesh. All members of the group are superb winter keepers, either in the crisper drawer of the refrigerator or—as we prefer—in damp sand in a cold, frost-free place. As such, they provide variety to the winter diet, eaten raw, sliced thin and salted (as Germans prefer, with beer), or boiled briefly and buttered (as Pepys had them at William Penn's) or in any way that turnips may be used in soups and stews. In none of these ways, however, are they quite like what one usually expects in a radish, for though early frosts and winter storage sweeten their flesh and cooking gentles it, they are still rather more biting and "horseradishy" than their late-spring and early-summer cousins, particularly when eaten raw.

Though when we first began vegetable gardening, only 'Black Spanish' and cultivars of daikon radish could be had, in recent years many varieties have become available from specialty seed growers. 'Black Spanish' is still the one we grow, however, for it has established a certain loyalty in us. Despite its wrinkled skin, approximately the color and texture of the sole of a worn sneaker, its flesh is white and not too peppery, and it holds its form and texture well when cooked. Unlike late-spring and early-summer radishes, it may be seeded quite late, usually around the Fourth of July, to make handsome, foot-tall coarse plants, and globes (if one plants the spherical rather than the sausage-shaped types) about the size of a small orange. Some are eaten fresh in late summer, but most are lifted for storage around the period of the first frosts in September. Stored in damp sand, they will keep well into the following spring, and even, in late winter, produce wan leaves in the dark that are a pleasant, only slightly pungent, addition to winter salads. Mostly the globes end up quartered, with small potatoes, carrots, cipollini onions or shallots, and a clove of garlic, as a component of Parchment-Baked Winter Roots.

For all its homely ingredients, this is a surprisingly elegant and delicious dish. For each serving, a foot-long piece of baker's parchment is torn off, and one or two vegetables of each sort piled on one side with salt, pepper, and a generous pat of butter. A sprig of fresh rosemary is nice if one keeps a plant through the winter; otherwise, a dusting of dried leaves will do. The parchment is then folded over the vegetables and crimped tightly by twirling both ends and tying them with kitchen twine. The packages, one per guest, are then placed on a baking sheet in a single layer and roasted in a moderate oven until the vegetables are done. (It is a good idea to make an extra, for testing.) The vegetables are served in their package (which takes on a beautiful, burnished color) either as a simple first course or with steak, lamb, chicken, or roast beef. When each individual package is torn open, a cloud of

⚑ *Radicchio, a choice, purple-leaved form of chickory, develops rapidly in cool spring weather, though slugs must be fought off from eating it if one would oneself. In hot gardens, it is only a spring crop, but in Vermont, it will stand well into early summer, when its heads, by then too bitter perhaps for salads, may be brushed with olive oil and grilled on an open fire.*

rich aromas will be released. The sturdy and comforting sustenance Parchment-Baked Winter Roots offers in the depths of January is very far from the lightness and freshness one craves in high spring. Though it is not a dish one wants in spring, vegetable gardening requires the gardener to plan, in the midst of one season, for what is to come. Thus, each season is perforce a layering into the next, both in plans and in anticipation.

But what we mostly crave in high summer is salad, and as succulent green leaves are its principal component, we return to the vegetable garden about a week or so after radishes are sown,

🪶 *A few nasturtiums should always be sown among the early lettuces, not only for their beauty but also for the pungent, water-cress flavor they add to salads. Once sown, they will appear in subsequent years as "volunteers" here and there. They resent transplanting, but young plants that have sprouted in the wrong place may be nipped off for additions to early salads.*

to put in the seed of the first leaf crops. We grow radicchio, which stands well in our cool summers and may be counted on to contribute its otherwise dollars-per-head burgundy elegance and sharp bitterness to salads from midsummer well into autumn. The oddly pungent, "meat" taste of arugula is sometimes a nice addition, sometimes a necessity, and rows of it are seeded from high spring to late summer, at two-week intervals, for a crop we are sure to have just when we want it. Endive, both smooth and frizzled, has become an erratic presence in markets, and as we like both types, either fresh in a salad or lightly cooked with white beans and sausage, short rows of each are also sown. Parsley must be on hand for all uses, and always we plant a row or two of nasturtiums for their gaiety in the garden and as an addition—flowers, young leaves, or extending shoots—to any salad.

But it is lettuces that primarily concern us. We always plant too many, for in spring, the rows are open and ready, and the names—'Rossa di Trentino,' 'Reine des Glaces,' 'Deer Tongue,' 'Oak Leaf,' 'Merveille de Quatres Saisons,' 'Red Sails'—make over-ordering and overseeding a thing not easily resisted. All our lettuces are sown rather thickly, with seeds almost touching, in the expectation that the seedlings, when they have achieved two or more true leaves, will be thinned by easing them from the row between the first and second fingers of one's hand, formed into a narrow V and pressed firmly on the ground, so as not to disturb their neighbors, which will then mature further without check and in their turn be tossed into the salad bowl. The ideal, of course, is to end up with a row of neatly spaced plants, perhaps eight inches one from the other, that will then form full heads of mature leaves. That is the ideal, and any overcast day, with the promise of a light drizzle or, better, its arrival will find us, per-

haps in bathing trunks, lifting plugs of seedlings from congested rows and transplanting them, neatly spaced, into fresh ones, for the pleasure to come of perfect heads.

But it is a unique thing about lettuces, among all the garden crops we can think of, that at each stage of their early growth they offer particular pleasures, first as tiny plants, when they are so delicate and fragile that only the merest whisper of dressing is called for, to juvenile leaves that hold their own in a mixed salad without being confused in the general mass, to mature leaves so crunchy and full of lettuceness that they may stand alone, not torn up into bits, and eaten with a stronger dressing, and even with perhaps an admixture of rich gravy from the previous course, preferably with one's fingers. (Curiously, only unmarried women, we are told by Renaissance books of etiquette, were permitted to do that, as when Cleopatra says in Shakespeare's *Antony and Cleopatra*, "My salad days, When I was young in judgment. . . ." What unmarried gentlemen did is open to question.) Even as mature plants that have gone to flower and seed, lettuces are at least visually splendid, and we always leave a few, by design or accident, for their beautifully symmetrical towers of growth. When they become shabby (or the space is needed for other crops) they are thrown to the chickens and the geese, who are, in their love of greens, more gourmand than we.

Each year we try new varieties of lettuce, as each year's catalog offerings tempt us with wonderful names and promises of finer colors, more heat resistance, more subtle flavors. About flavor, however, we are a little skeptical, for all lettuces seem to taste more or less lettucey, perhaps a little more bitter or a little less. It is the texture of a lettuce that is important, and all are nice, provided they are never fibrous or tough. So we

❧ *We sow almost all lettuces thickly, hoping to harvest them as "thinnings" or to transplant them to waiting rows where they may develop full heads. For it is a nice characteristic of lettuce that it is palatable at almost any stage, even the mature and bitter heads in a cold soup.*

plant a range, from the fragile, silky 'Oak Leaf' or 'Deer Tongue' to the sturdier "salad bowl" or Boston types, to the upright, crunchy substance of the romaines. We have even flirted, in recent years, with iceberg types, since, if one wants a chiffonade for any reason (even for childhood memory), they are without compare for that.

One variety, however, stays constant in our choices, and that is 'Black Seeded Simpson.' First introduced in 1870, it is still the benchmark, in our opinion, against which all garden lettuces should be judged. We have no idea who Mr. Simpson was (though we are grateful), but we do know that the seed is in fact black, as opposed to the gray-white of most other lettuce cultivars. Among lettuces, which are easy for us to grow all

season in our cool, mountain garden, it is the easiest of all, germinating reliably and producing an abundant crop that is usable, from first seedling almost to bolted plant. Interesting salads are best built in the garden, taking a bit of this and a bit of that into the trug. But 'Black Seeded Simpson,' which we always have in abundance, is the foundation layer, a sturdy beginning. Its leaves are very beautiful, nicely quilted and a clear, chartreuse green, so beautiful in fact that were it not an edible crop, one might still grow it in the flower garden, for the pale, fresh elegance of its leaves, which would enhance any other color, say, the clear blue of Petunia 'Azure Pearls,' or the vivid scarlet of *Lychnis chalcedonica* (Maltese cross). People do that, and Rosalind Creasy has

High Spring

69

written a splendid book (*The Complete Book of Edible Landscaping*) about how it and other vegetables may be combined with flowers to wonderfully decorative effect. We still keep our 'Black Seeded Simpson' and our cabbages, leeks, purple orach, and celery firmly within the bounds of our vegetable garden. For though they are all handsome plants that might grace mixed plantings of vegetables and flowers, there is a special pleasure, in any season, in going into the vegetable garden, and it is quite different from the pleasure of entering the perennial or rock garden, or the wooded rhododendron walk. We prefer to keep it pure.

We like our lettuces sown in individual rows in single varieties, for then one has the pleasure of enjoying their various shapes and colors, and their textures, silky to crunchy, can be combined in a nice blend, perhaps with other greens, no two of which will have precisely the same character when they come to the table—the assertive leaves of young arugula, the tips of purple orach, a little lemon-acid sorrel, some dark-green spinach, a nip of parsley or a few nasturtium blossoms—to create salads as one harvests.

But we compromise with mesclun, a sort of salad already built on the ground. Lettuce is the principal component of all mesclun mixes, of which many are now offered by seed houses; and indeed, it never hurts, if one has a few lonely lettuce seeds left in a packet, to compromise the make up of the mix by throwing them in. But beyond lettuces are many other curious things:

Saint Barbara's weed, miner's lettuce and land cress, arugula, orach, purslane, and many other "weeds" that appear in the thicket of growth. All are delicious, having more or less peppery pungence according to the mix one chooses. The culture of mesclun, however, will be a stretch for the American gardener, set in his or her ways and used to spacing seed with nice exactness along the row. For unlike other common garden salad crops, mesclun is sown very thickly in hand-sized depressions along the row, as thickly, perhaps, as "hairs on the dog's back." The crowded, immature plants are snipped off with scissors when they have reached a height of about four inches. From basal stumps, the various plants will make new growth, which can be clipped again, and perhaps again for three croppings. After that, the tiny plants have generally given their all and should be turned under to clear the way for the seeding of something else, or perhaps for a fresh seeding of mesclun. The results, in the salad bowl, are frankly addictive, speaking at once of peasant thrift and extreme sophistication. Mesclun, unknown to us when we first began as vegetable gardeners, was for centuries a way, throughout the Mediterranean and in southern France, of making use of odd bits of land in the vegetable plot, and mesclun is now for sale, at many dollars a pound, in good gourmet and even supermarkets. Thus, as with so many other activities—the raising of vegetables, particularly—simple, ancient practice and modern chic unexpectedly meet. About that, no comment need be made except that we are glad.

For lettuce or mesclun, however, or even for a decent radish, we must wait almost a month after our first seedings, which is to say, almost to the beginning of May. Fortunately, however, our hunger for green things rich in vitamins may be satisfied elsewhere than in the vegetable garden. For in all parts of North America—in woods,

❧ LEFT: *Lettuces are tidy, attractive plants, and so they may be used to line paths or planted as an ornamental fringe around quadrant beds, within which untidier plants such as bush beans or potatoes may be grown. Here, 'Black Seeded Simpson,' a nonpareil for us, makes an elegant chartreuse border beneath a standard Pee-Gee hydrangea.*

❧ *It is always good to have a patch of sorrel in the garden, put to the side where it will not be disturbed, as it is a winter-hardy perennial. It is good in soups, though with cooking it generally becomes an unattractive mud color. Better, perhaps, to throw a few of its acid, vinegary leaves into an early salad.*

streambeds, fields, abandoned pastures, dreadfully disturbed land, and even backyards, lawns, and gardens—healthful food abounds. Many people have known how to garner this wealth, in a chain of knowledge that extends from prehistoric times to the present. For Native Americans, the gathering of wild greens was an absolute necessity, correcting the vitamin deficiencies of a winter diet of fat-rich game and dried meats. They passed their knowledge on to the first colonists, who were mostly subsistence farmers, not averse to tossing this or that weed into the pot. The knowledge was preserved among New England farm folk (and those of their race that pushed farther south and west), so it was not extraordinary, in such households, to be served a dish of dandelion greens, raw as a salad but

dressed with hot bacon grease and a little cider vinegar, or cooked with salted meat in "pot likker." In early spring there might also be a side dish of ramps (*Allium tricoccum*) gathered from the wild in damp woods where little else but ferns would grow. Gold-rush miners of the mid-nineteenth century eagerly sought miner's lettuce (*Montia perfoliata*) as a cure for scurvy, and it was not hard to find growing along damp streambeds

❧ RIGHT: *Mesclun, whatever the blend, is merely an assortment of tasty roadside weeds with some lettuce thrown in. So it is worth knowing that if the packet of seed is meager (and expensive), whatever one has left over of any lettuce after its row has been sown can be added for greater bulk. A "cut-and-come-again" crop, mesclun is sown very thickly, and always clipped with scissors, to regrow for subsequent harvests.*

from Montana to California, or wherever the miners' patient and tedious work occurred.

With the increasing urbanization of North America in the forties and fifties, however, a knowledge of foraging for wild foods was largely lost. People who knew how to do it belonged to certain ethnic groups ("*Those people*," the dismissive culture of our childhoods would have had it) or were numbered among cranks and oddballs who wore sandals in winter, sang songs together for other than religious purposes, "were not married," and went mostly unshaven and unshorn. Among the latter group, the late Euell Gibbons was a sort of hero, though all his pictures show him to have been a quite ordinary-looking and presentable sort of guy. Still, his landmark work, *Stalking the Wild Asparagus* (1962), reminded Americans that there was a small and very interesting window of freedom from supermarket produce raised in the deserts of California and force-fed with chemicals. On a deeper level, Gibbons insisted that gathering one's own food, or at least some of it, contained a spiritual value, reconnecting us with nature and the long evolution of our species.

Certainly, were Gibbons alive today, he would be amused by how clearly his message was heard, not perhaps in the average American home, but by gourmet cooks and fashionable restaurants, which now routinely include salads of "wild greens" on the menu, garnished often with roadside flowers—daylilies, red clover, or limpid-blue chickory. There is now even a small but thriving agricultural industry that raises native and naturalized plants previously gathered from the wild (and available there still for free) to supply the demands of expensive restaurants.

We have gathered wild greens for salads as long as we have lived in Vermont, and each year our repertory increases, as, we presume, does our

health and well-being. Still, we would offer a word of caution to anyone who chooses to gather food from the wild. The plants we suggest for gathering have all been eaten by many peoples, over centuries of time. They may all be considered part of our heritage, though few of them are commonly cultivated as agricultural crops, at least in this country. But even common and generally healthful cultivated vegetables, such as carrots or sweet potatoes, can prove toxic in large quantities; and there are people who become deathly ill from any wheat product, though to most of us it is the staff of life. It is true, too, that many foods gathered from the wild may be seriously contaminated with road salts, fuel residues, and heavy metals, agricultural chemicals, or the feces of wild animals. All this is not to say that wild foods should not be gathered, but only that one should choose the location of one's harvest carefully, and consume in moderation, at least until one's tolerance is determined. It should be said, too, that all the plants we recommend for gathering are common weeds—even "serious" weeds—and so they may be harvested with a free conscience, stealing from no man nor from Nature herself.

Among wild salad greens, our great favorite is the lowly chickweed, *Stellaria media*. Occurring now wherever land has been cultivated, its actual origins are in doubt, though probably it began its worldwide pilgrimage in southern Europe, where it is still harvested in quantity from beneath the trees in olive and citrus orchards. An annual plant (and an abundant self-seeder), it will make a delicate green haze over moist, fertile ground, in sun or part shade, and it seems particularly to relish damp, sour city soils. Many lax, watery stems are produced from a central root, and the arrow-shaped leaves enlarge progressively until they reach about half an inch in length. Then the plant flowers, producing many tiny grayish-white stars—hence the genus name, *Stellaria*. Never much more than a foot in height, chickweed is best harvested by clipping its stems with sharp scissors, taking leaves and tiny flowers all together. The plant will then regrow, much as mesclun does, producing another crop. Its flavor, which is bland and "lettuce-y," makes an excellent support to more pungent greens in a mixed salad.

Similar to chickweed in flavor is jewelweed, *Impatiens capensis*. Were it not one of the worst weeds gardeners have to deal with, it would be a treasured plant, for it is quite beautiful in all its parts. An annual of very quick growth, it produces fat, many-branched fleshy stems with cool green leaves an inch or two long, and thumb-sized "snapdragons" in high summer, usually yellow overspotted with orange freckles, though variants appear that are brick red, cream, or pink. Native from Newfoundland to Georgia, it can attain five feet by summer's end, producing large stands in damp woods and the shadier sides of country roads. Asian species of *Impatiens* have long been treasured in Chinese medicine as a treatment for inflamed wounds and skin diseases, and *I. capensis* inherits these properties, as woodsmen know who crush its stems and leaves to neutralize the effects of poison ivy or to alleviate the sting of nettles. As a salad plant, jewelweed should be harvested when it is no more than six inches high, taking leaf tips and succulent stems together. Its season is brief, hardly more than two weeks. After that, the plant develops concentrations of calcium oxalate crystals that are not healthful to some people in quantity. In any case, jewelweed should always be eaten in moderation, just a handful of young leafy stems thrown into a mixed salad.

No such caution need be offered for dandelions (*Taraxacum officinale*), every part of which has been recognized as healthful since the Romans first cultivated it in their gardens. Its new young leaves may be used either raw in salads or cooked as a potherb. Immature flower buds can be pickled as a substitute to capers, and fully expanded blossoms make a fine, dry white wine. The white, fleshy roots may be parched and ground as a substitute for coffee, much in the manner of a close relative, the widely naturalized roadside weed chicory, *Cichorium intybus*. The name "dandelion" is pretty in itself, an old English corruption of the French *dent de lion*, "lion's tooth," a recognition of its toothed, or dentate, leaves. But most modern French people know it by a blunter name, *piss en lit*, attesting to the fact that it is a gentle diuretic, stimulating the kidneys in a healthful way while not robbing the body of potassium.

The country people among whom we have lived for over twenty years hardly know these facts, at least not any but the most obvious of them. Still, they anticipate dandelion season with pleasure, recognizing in the first sprouting leaves their richness in minerals and in vitamins C and A, a welcomed spring tonic after a winter of canned goods and supermarket produce. Dandelions may be harvested in spring as early as they appear, usually mid- to late March in Vermont, when even five bright days shining on the newly thawed ground will cause them to form rosettes of two-inch-long leaves. Harvesting continues for a month or more, even after the fat buttons of bud have formed in the center of the plant, but it terminates when the first full-blown flowers appear, after which the leaves are too bitter to be palatable.

As the dandelion season nicely coincides with the first serious weeding of the garden, one can gather them with double pleasure, clearing the flower beds and the lawn of weeds and at the same time accumulating a dish of fresh greens for dinner. There is a craft to the harvest, however, for the cook (even when it is we ourselves) will be rightly discouraged by a trug of dirty leaves, roots, and fragments of winter detritus. Dandelions are true perennials, growing for many years from the same root, and even regenerating in clumps when a bit of that root is left underground. So if one is weeding, all of the roots must be grubbed out; in waste places, for salad leaves only a bit of the crown need be taken by a flick of a sharp knife, just below where the leaves meet the thick, carrotlike root. Either way, gather the fresh new spring leaves in one hand, fold back the old ones with the other, and sever what one intends to use just above the crown juncture. Clean leaves can then be taken to the kitchen, plunged in cold water to relieve them of sand, spun or patted dry, and thrown into the pot or salad bowl.

It may be that dandelions, for those who were not born to them, are an acquired taste, described as bitter (with a wrinkle of the nose) by those who never learned to like them and "tonic" by those who do. In any case, they have a "chew" to them, pleasant to many people, but rather like eating hay to others. So they gain by being combined with sweeter and more tender greens, of which various members of the genus *Viola* are the best. All are edible in leaf or flower, from cultivated forms such as pansies, violas, and garden violets, to woodland and meadow species, some of which are native and many happily naturalized. Their pretty blossoms are favorites of cooks who like to garnish salads and pastries with flowers, but most of the flavor, such as it is, is in the leaves, and certainly all of the vitamins, particularly vitamin C, with which violet leaves are rich. Still, they are bland in flavor, like delicate lettuces when young, a "carrier" for stronger fla-

vors and an interesting contrast in shape and color to other greens. All *Viola* species seem to benefit from shearing and the picking of their flowers, as those of us know whose first garden task was deadheading the pansies. So, from cultivated plants or from fields and woods, one can take leaves and blossoms in spring with a clear conscience, leaving the stems and fibrous or rhysotomous roots to produce another crop.

For more pungence, Saint Barbara's weed, *Barbarea vulgaris,* should be eagerly sought wherever it grows. A member of the mustard family, it originated in Europe but was brought by the first colonists to North America as a garden vegetable, where it escaped to become widely naturalized in all but the warmest and driest parts of the continent. The feast of Saint Barbara occurs on December 4, and the genus name of the plant attests to its great hardiness, since it was the only green thing that could be gathered in the depths of winter. But whenever a plant has been treasured for centuries, it accrues many popular names, and so *Barbarea vulgaris* has been variously called wintercress, upland cress, land cress, yellow rocket, scurvy grass, and simply wild mustard by old New Englanders. As a cultivated plant it is a boon to vegetable gardeners in colder climates, since it may be sown in late summer and harvested in very early spring, long before the hardiest spring crops—radishes and spinach and peas—may be planted. But it is so plentiful as a "weed" that it need not be cultivated at all, but taken freely from the wild wherever it grows.

Barbarea vulgaris is a handsome plant, as weeds go, producing from a central, weakly perennial crown a rosette of artfully crafted leaves, with two to eight pairs of small lateral lobes along the stem and a much larger lobe at the end. Leaves are smooth and shiny, lacking the hairiness that many people find disagreeable in other members of the mustard family. It favors any damp spot, and flourishes along the verges of ditches and streambeds, in wet meadows, and even in neglected areas of the vegetable and flower garden where the soil is moist. It is best harvested as early in spring as it appears, from mid-March to mid-April in Vermont, after which the leaves may become too pungent and peppery, though the foot-high flower stems, appearing in May here, may be picked to add an accent of daffodil yellow to a mixed salad.

Pungence of a different sort can be added to any spring salad by mints, of which many forms are grown in herb gardens as rampageous perennials, valued as additions to cooling summer drinks, used sometimes as a cooked flavoring herb, and put up as mint sauce to accompany roast lamb. We use mint for all these purposes, but they are most valuable to us as spring greens added to a mixed salad. When used that way, they are best when the shoots are only three or four inches high, and as the plants are so extremely vigorous of increase, it never hurts to pinch out a few tips. Only mildly minty at that stage, with much less bite than mature summer leaves possess, a few young shoots add a pleasant undertone to salads. It seems hardly to matter at that stage which mint one chooses, whether spearmint, peppermint, apple mint, or any wild variety one recognizes not by name but by the fragrance it releases as one walks through wild places.

Though on a mild day in spring it is pleasant to take a light basket on one's arm and go for a long walk, garnering whatever the fields, woods, and streams offer, the best foraging is probably close to home, around the flower and vegetable garden, where many early-developing weeds are most abundant and tasty. The fattest, finest dandelions will certainly be plentiful there, and vio-

lets, and possibly Saint Barbara's weed. Chickweed will never be far from any recently cultivated ground, and if you have succeeded in keeping jewelweed out of the shadier parts of your garden, we would like to know your secret. But in the garden, other edible plants will be available, all familiar nuisances, many worth gathering for food.

Purslane (*Portulaca oleracea*) is among the commonest, easiest to recognize, and most delicious. Of Indian and Eurasian origins, it has been cultivated for over two thousand years, and is now what botanists call "cosmopolitan," having naturalized happily anywhere gardening has occurred. It was Gandhi's favorite vegetable, and it is still much cultivated throughout the world, both in its small, green-leafed variety in the larger, yellow-leaved form. It can hardly be called an escapee from gardens, for it is always happiest in them, growing with a fine sense of irony next to a fashionable and expensive mesclun mix, or among the various greens with which it will probably be included. It grows easily in any sunny spot, too easily some would say, for it can reproduce not only from seed (which is abundant) but also from bits of stem that take root along the ground, even when severed from the mother plant, and from its fleshy leaves, which can root and regrow infant plants wherever they fall. So much the better, when one comes to relish its crunchy, succulent stems and leaves, lettuce-y but with an undertone of pepper and lemon; and of course, so much the worse if one doesn't. When we have great bunches of it, usually from a vigorous early-summer weeding, we prepare it like spinach for an excellent cooked vegetable. But a few young stems with their leaves are always a nice addition to any salad, distinct in texture, form, and taste.

Purslane comes late for a spring salad, apt as

it is to reach perfection only when hot weather (hot for us in Vermont) arrives in early summer. But orach (*Atriplex hortensis*) will pepper the ground with young seedlings by early May, and will be large enough to be worth gathering shortly thereafter. Comparisons with other plants, particularly for culinary use, can often be fanciful, but in the case of orach, the common name "mountain spinach" seems entirely accurate, since it may be used in any way spinach can, raw or cooked, and is a great deal easier to grow. It has a long history in gardens, having been cultivated by the Romans, grown in England and northern European gardens since the Middle Ages, and brought by the first colonists to North America, where its value was quickly recognized by Native Americans. Often called saltbush (though it is no bush at all, but rather a quick-growing hardy annual), it was treasured for the quality it has to season and make flavorful other greens. Though now seldom seen in gardens, orach is pure ease to grow, for once it has been sown and allowed to develop in any garden, it will reappear in very early spring, particularly on the trodden ground of vegetable garden paths. Most plants will be taken from there as weedings for salads, though a few should always be left in convenient places, or transplanted into a row, for repeat pickings of mature leaves throughout the summer and to provide seed for next year's harvest. Mature plants, particularly of the red-leaved variety, are very handsome, achieving a height of four to five feet at maturity. That variety bears the rather cumbersome name of *Atriplex hortensis* var. *atrosanguinea* c.v. 'Rubra,' but if one wishes to grow orach at all, it is the one to search out, since its dusty beet-red leaves are so beautiful in salads and in the garden.

Despite the missionary zeal of Euell Gibbons in the late fifties and sixties, and despite the fact that many expensive restaurants now serve mixed wild greens on their menus, the gathering of food from the wild or from chance seedings of weeds in the garden is apt to be a new adventure for most American gardeners and cooks. In southern and central Europe, however, such gatherings are taken for granted, but still eagerly anticipated, as a sort of sport and a holiday romp in the country. Elderly relatives pass on to young children the knowledge of what is good and not good to pick for eating, as has been the way of our species from its earliest beginnings. Around Rome, where wild greens have been valued for over two thousand years, sophisticated diners consider themselves cheated if their salad of wild greens, *misticanza,* does not contain at least twenty-one separate varieties. Do they count them, we wonder, shape by shape and texture by texture and taste by taste? Still, the point is well taken, for part of the pleasure of any wild salad is composing the dish outdoors, clipping a bit of this or that, throwing in this texture or flavor or color to balance or add variety to all the others. No wild salad ought to be of any one thing, unless, indeed, of dandelions, when one is really hungry for them; rather, it should be a sort of edible bouquet, at once as varied and beautiful as it is salubrious.

But though the fields, woods, and streambeds command our attention, drawing us to themselves like magnets after our long, housebound winter and providing us with the finest and freshest things we have then to eat, at the highest point of high spring one other crop demands our attention. For around mid- to late April, depending on the weather, peas must be put into the ground. Though other crops in their season—fine lettuces and radishes, green beans, tomatoes ripened on the vine, or fresh-picked corn—justify the vegetable garden and all the labor it entails, peas, really fresh peas picked at the briefest second of perfection, seem to us almost the garden's entire reason for being. Even if the inevitable contractions of age force us to give up the growing of many crops, we'll still grow peas. For, like corn's, the sugars in peas convert to starch within minutes of picking, and peas bought in the pod from the supermarket will scarcely be superior to any package of them taken from the frozen-food locker, and possibly vastly inferior. When well grown, peas are almost the most beautiful of garden crops, their neatly trained vines—like those of tomatoes, pole beans, and cucumbers—contributing commanding structure in the garden. For all these reasons, we'll stay with peas, for as long as we can.

It must be said, however, that growing good peas is not easy, and that among garden crops, they are the least productive or, if not that, are second only to corn in low productivity per plant. (Silvia Thompson has calculated, in her excellent book *The Kitchen Garden* [Bantam Books, 1995], that it takes about twenty-five plants to yield a little more than a cup of shelled peas.) Fortunately, however, though each vine will yield at most five pods, and some less, peas are peculiar in that they like to grow very close together. So unlike other garden crops, which must be evenly spaced one from another for maximum yield, peas are sown not in a neat single row, but in a shallow, hand-width furrow with the seeds almost touching. This is great luck, not only because it prevents those who really love peas from putting the whole garden down to them, but also because it makes simpler—somewhat simpler—the real burden of growing peas, which is providing adequate support for their climbing vines. Peas have been developed into "bush," or stakeless, forms, and we have tried some, once or twice. But they still sprawled in an

undisciplined way along the ground, and we had trouble finding the ripe pods. Mice and slugs did not, so those we succeeded in harvesting were sad nibbled things, usually past their prime. In any case, such plants have been bred largely for the convenience of the modern canning industry, where flavor is the last consideration. The whole point of peas is their flavor. So one is stuck with vines—actually, the taller the better—and so with the necessity to stake them.

In the beginning we were very romantic about staking, thinking that our vegetable garden, a somewhat antique venture anyway, should look as much like nineteenth-century English and French gardens as possible. "Pea stakes" were therefore the thing, made of twiggy brush put by from autumn or spring prunings of the ornamental garden, or gathered from fields where shrubby growth was coppiced each year for such purposes. At the start, we had lots of "shrubby growth," as our garden began with the felling of trees for space and light and there were always good, branchy tops of beech or maple to be cut from the burn pile. But cutting it into convenient six-foot lengths, hauling it from the woods to the garden, inserting each twiggy stick into the ground, and tying all of them together into neat rows, made us feel that though peas might be worth any amount of trouble, certain pictorial effects were not.

We then had to resort to lengths of chicken wire stapled to cedar posts dug in at six-foot intervals along the row. When rusted down from its fresh, shiny silver, chicken wire still had a nice country feel to it, and the posts gave a sense of sturdiness and permanence. It was an illusory sense, for peas, like most garden crops, should not be grown in the same rows two years running, and so the posts and chicken wire had to be rolled up each autumn and

❧ *Most surely, peas are the queen of the late-spring and early-summer garden. After years of frustrating experiments (sometimes elegant, sometimes ugly), we have abandoned rustic poles and chicken wire for bamboo stakes and black plastic netting. The results are both easier and tidier, though we admit that some of the country-garden charm (as in this picture) has fled.*

repositioned each spring. It was devil's work, for though putting the structures down was relatively easy the first time, repositioning them was not. The work required two of us, one to hold the first post straight while the other, chicken wire draped around his shoulder, dug in the second, and so on. Curses were plentiful. And the results, after the first year, were hardly attractive, for the wire sagged and bowed with each year's handling, and the posts were seldom straight. The vines, also, perversely leaned away from the perpendicular, closing off the space between rows and requiring that they be looped back to the way they should grow with lengths of bailing twine.

Finally, we have come to another system, which we admit is a compromise with our aesthetic, and probably also with ecological morality. Taking a clue from the staking of tomatoes and cucumbers, we planted the peas in two parallel rows four feet apart, inserted eight-foot-tall bamboo stakes along the rows at four-foot intervals, and tied them in to a ridgepole running down the middle between the rows. The stakes were then clad with black plastic bird netting on both sides, tied to the poles with bailing twine. That is, of course, the compromise, for though the plastic net is almost invisible, and becomes entirely so when the vines have clothed it, it is still black plastic. Nor can it be reused from year to year, since tendrils and other pea bits weave back and forth through it, and cannot easily be cleaned away. So, though the stakes can be saved when the vines have completed their productivity, vines and plastic are bundled all together and taken to the dump. But the peas climb happily without encouragement on the slanted net, making handsome walls of glaucous blue-green leaves, and displaying their pods for easy harvest. One can even crawl within to gather the few that

dangle inside, a good thing if one is (as one is) pea-greedy.

One is told always that peas should be planted "as early in spring as the ground can be worked." In areas that experience brief springs followed by hot, dry early summers, that is perhaps good advice, as peas require very cool conditions and abundant moisture to make strong vegetative growth, and hence to produce a good crop. But in our garden, we never know how early "as early" might be, since thaws might come by the end of March, but the ground is still soggy, which pea seed hates, sooner rotting than sprouting. Frosts are also probable well to the end of April, and though pea seed and first seedlings are frost-hardy, tender growth is not. So, for pea seeding, the last week of April or the first of May is soon enough. But we realize we are lucky, in a sense, because cool, damp weather obtains here well into mid-June, and that is bliss for peas, however much it may discourage the growth of tomatoes or corn. Germination seems best when the seed is sown rather shallowly, not deeper than twice its own thickness, and as dense as you can make yourself sprinkle it in. (For this reason, it is always a good idea to order two packets of seed for a row you think will need only one.) Because of this shallow sowing, rains will sometimes expose germinating seed, or they may actually, in their leap to life, push themselves out of the ground. Never must one push them back in, for that will break the emerging root and the infant pea will perish. Rather, sprinkle a little loose soil from the edge of the row over them, rather like tucking an infant under a blanket. One should also keep an eye out for birds, who seem to relish a newly sprouted pea above all other things, and can gullet down a whole row in a surprisingly short time. At the first signs of such depredation, the row should be covered

❧ *Tropical, hot-season plants such as peppers, tomatoes, and eggplants wait until the very end of high spring and even early summer to be transplanted. But though the peppers have just been put in, the garden has already assumed the abundant luxuriance that will characterize it until a killing frost, more than two months away, comes to cut it down.*

with additional strips of black plastic netting (compromise again) held above the sprouting peas by small sticks. It can actually be left in place, for the peas will grow up through it, and once they have reached two true leaves, they no longer seem to be tempting to birds.

Specialty seed nurseries list many varieties of peas, and we have tried many, though we come back each year to one old standard. That is 'Tall Telephone,' almost indistinguishable from the nineteenth-century English variety 'Alderman.' Part of the reason we love it is that it makes very tall vines, eight feet at maturity, and if one goes to the trouble of putting up supports, as we do, then it is nice to have them clothed to the top. But the virtues of 'Tall Telephone' extend beyond that, in abundantly born, well-filled pods with eight peas in each, good flavor, and reasonable disease resistance. Nothing as important as peas, however, should rest on one variety, and so we also always plant 'Green Arrow' and 'Wando.' Both are sturdy old reliables, both semidwarf, which is to say that both will still need support, though only to four feet or so. 'Wando' is particularly desirable for its heat resistance, greater perhaps than that of any other variety grown.

All these varieties are both larger in vine and pea size than forms of *petits pois* that are considered most choice. We admit that there is something hugely appealing in having a dish of the smallest peas possible, each scarcely larger than a BB. So, though they are far more difficult to grow than standard varieties, and far less abundant in yield (it takes so many BBs to fill a dish!)

we always plant some of these choice midgets, the vines of which seldom reach four feet. Of the two varieties we know best, 'Précovelle' sounds appropriately French, and 'Waverex' does not; still, there seems little difference between them in yield, flavor, or tininess.

It is when the pea vines flower that high spring shifts into summer, and the vegetable garden is at its highest peak of beauty. There is beauty, certainly, at all seasons: in winter, when the skeletons of the standard currants and gooseberries, the espaliered apples, show clearest against the snow-covered rows, all pleated like seersucker; in early spring, when the rows, fecund and mellowed from their winter sleep, lie ready for the seeding of the first crops—radishes, lettuce, broad beans, and mesclun; in late spring, when neat green lines of sprouted seed give further definition to the rows and the promise of so many good things to come; in high summer, when the integrity of those rows, their pattern on the ground, is compromised by lush leaf and by sprawling stem, creating a maze to wander through; and in autumn, when frosts threaten, and all the work of the growing year must be hastily undone, stripping tomato vines, gathering potatoes, searching for squash and pumpkins, trundling all under cover in the hurried exhilaration of final harvest. But in high spring and early summer, when the pea vines produce their wan, white mothlike flowers, the garden is at perhaps its most beautiful. It is then, most certainly, that we know why we are here, and what we are doing.

Early Summer

At last. There are throughout the year holidays of greater or lesser weight in human lives: Christmas, the New Year, spring's first day, the Fourth of July, birthdays—all marking some moment of attainment or release, a cycle completed, a new beginning, a brief moment of fullness. But for us the most joyful day of the whole calendar is that one, whenever it comes, that marks the end of frost. Till that day, we play a game with nature, a kind of truth or dare, in which a spell of mildness teases us into a little trust, enough at least to risk sowing the very hardiest crops—radishes and turnips, peas, spinach, and onion sets. When a week or two passes and they are well up, we confidently follow with the slightly less hardy crops, trusting to the still-cold earth the brassicas in all their many forms, and potatoes, well sprouted already in the dark storage whence others have been departing all winter long for the pot. Vegetables are ranked in tiers according to their hardiness, but even with these first two tiers, we must hedge our bet with nature by keeping stacks of burlap handy, ready to cover the first sproutlings should we plunge again, even well into May, to nighttime lows in the mid-twenties.

It is all as wearing as the beginning of a love affair, full of hints and promises, teases, uncertainties, doubts. But eventually there comes an assurance, tied not so much to a specific date (though always after May 20 here) as to the behavior of fronts and air masses in Calgary and Hudson Bay, and the responses of certain "weather" plants in the garden: the swelling of maple buds, snowdrops, forsythia, apple blossoms. The weather has settled, and the last of winter's air has quite drained away from the North. We have entered a frost-free world, and our brief span of summer is about to begin.

Stacked on the hall table for weeks now have been all the seeds we lustfully acquired in January and February. The packets are still mostly neat, untorn, and unmuddied, with magical names and all the hope of the coming season still on them. With the progressive warming of our world, the stack loses its tidiness and decreases in height, as the hardiest seeds are entrusted to the cold ground and the packet generally returns to the table smudged and restapled, with a few seeds left in it for an emergency backup or a late-summer sowing. Left behind are the true tropicals, children not of northern Europe or the high Andes but of the jungles and savannahs of the southern latitudes, places where the earth warms early and frosts come, if at all, only in the depths of winter. In their abundance, those still-unopened packets are a caution, reminding us that in our first enthusiastic sowings of radishes and turnips, lettuce and peas, carrots, onions and all the brassicas, we must leave room for these lovers of heat and high summer, and—by sad paradox—also of space. After all, they are for the most part Native Americans.

Beans, corn, and squash make up the Holy Trinity of gifts to our table from warmer parts of the American continent. All three are incredibly quick of growth, and are so anciently associated with humanity that their diversity and adaptability are ensured. They flourish even here in Vermont, closer to the Arctic than to their temperate homes, producing abundantly in summers far briefer than those where they first grew. After so many generations of selection, first by Native Americans and then by Europeans to whom they were early introduced, each of the three exists in a dizzying plethora of forms and varieties, more than enough to furnish the average home garden many times over. It is a never-ending richness, the deepest Christmas stocking that ever was. And though we have favorites to which we return faithfully every year, we still cannot resist ordering forms new to us, though usually of ancient lineage, in a never-ending degustation of bean, squash, and corn.

In their abundance, ease of cultivation, and adaptability to space, beans are perhaps the best. Or worst. We always grow too many beans. How, in January, can we resist names like 'Dragon Tongue,' 'Fin des Bagnols,' 'Triomphe de Farcy,' 'Jacob's Cattle,' 'Trionfo Violetto,' 'Painted Lady,' or 'Midnight Black Turtle'? When the packets are cut open and the seed shaken out into the hand, the magic continues, in shapes elegantly thin (like Good n' Plenty) or as roundly packaged as a tortoise. Colors range from pure white and cream through taupe and beige and brown, to Cherokee red and black; some are streaked, speckled, spotted, or eyed with one color over another. The idea of any seed is thrilling, a potent, compact repository of dormant life waiting on the gardener's whim and the forces of nature to spring into existence, wax large, and reproduce. Beans are peculiarly irresistible, falling so easily into the hand and as easily picked out, one by one, for perfect spacing in shallow, arrow-straight trenches formed by pressing the handle of a rake into the newly fluffed soil. Large as they are, it is easy to tell the top of a bean from the bottom, and since the root will emerge from the "eye" side, it seems courteous to plant each seed with that side down, just to make things simple in the beginning. All this makes it very easy to order more varieties than we can plant, and to plant more than we can eat. It is fortunate then that we can give away the excess to friends, who have come to count on it as have we, for it frees us from the guilt of imaginative overindulgence.

Still, we do not count it as luck that one bean will not grow well for us. Limas, of which we are both hugely fond, have consistently let us down, failing to set pods here in Vermont. Being tender, heat-loving plants of tropical American origin, they germinate poorly in our cold spring soils, and the coolness of our nights, delightful to us and to many plants, completely discourages them. So for lima beans, we make an exception to what is almost a perfect rule, and depend on the frozen-food locker of the local supermarket. (We once read an interview with Julia Child, in which she confessed to the same indulgence, and that made us feel much better about it.)

Though there is no real substitute for lima beans, soybeans come close, particularly a cultivar called 'Butter Bean,' offered by Johnny's Select Seed in Albion, Maine. For us it has produced abundantly, and has somewhat quieted our regret for all those years of failed limas. Perhaps, however, it does soybeans an injustice to think of them as mere compensation; for shelled, boiled,

and dressed with butter, they are a good enough thing in themselves, as, we have heard, is rattlesnake meat (which, for ease of going down, is endlessly compared to chicken). Even better is to prepare and eat soybeans in the Japanese way (*edamame*), by boiling the young pods unshelled until the beans inside are just tender, and serving them in their shells either tepid or cold, as a first course that will occupy and amuse guests while other good things are coming on. They are as addictive as pistachio nuts, but a great deal more healthful.

Soybeans are an occasional and pleasant treat, but most of the space we have for the cultivation of beans is given over to the bush and pole sorts that, in their season, almost define the summer diet. Bush beans bear earlier than climbing sorts, usually between fifty-five and sixty days from sowing. They are easy, flexible plants for the garden, maturing at only a little more than a foot in height, fitting nicely into rows or at the edges of square or rectangular beds. Being bred to be squat, they never climb, though some older varieties may attempt a wayward shoot or two. When it is their time to bear, they do it all at once, producing thick clusters of down-hanging pods until they give up from exhaustion. Daily picking is required, not so much to maintain productivity (for each plant seems to have its quota, beyond which it is unprepared to go) as to secure beans of the finest flavor, not so small as to be tasteless nor so large as to be tough, mealy, or stringy. Though in theory one could stagger their sowing, or plant quicker- and slower-maturing varieties all at once, our experience at this northern latitude is that all the beans one sows will perversely come in at about the same time, resulting in a daily glut. At first, of course, that is a phenomenon to be welcomed, as we remember how many months have elapsed since we last

enjoyed fresh beans. For with them, as with almost all other vegetable foods, we keep to a strict seasonality. Our bush beans begin to crop in mid-July and continue through to late August. We keep up with them as best we can. But though they freeze easily, and the result, for a frozen food, is quite good, we still prefer to eat them during the eight or ten weeks when they are in season.

Bush beans are remarkable in their diversity, but may be grouped into four principal types: round green ones (including purple, which turn green when cooked), flat-podded sorts, yellow wax beans, and very slender French, or filet, beans. Of the four, the round ones are least remarkable in flavor, least definitive of essential beanness. But they may be sown earlier than the others, particularly the purple-podded sorts such as 'Trionfo Violetto' or 'Royal Burgundy,' which may go into cold ground a full two weeks earlier than any other bean and still germinate reliably and crop within fifty-one days of sowing. They are all very prolific bearers, and though the first and finest may require no more preparation than a quick boil or steaming, some salt and pepper, and a pat of butter, older, more mature beans will benefit by a bit of elaboration. The best treatment we know is to leave the beans whole, soak them for thirty minutes or so in cold water, drain them, and toss them all at once into a large iron pot in which about a tablespoon of olive oil has been heated almost to smoking. The beans are

then stirred more or less continuously until they become limp and tender, but still preserve some crispness within. Just before serving, a tablespoon or two of soy sauce is thrown in and stirred about to coat them. The result is surprisingly flavorful, closer to a grilled or roasted vegetable than to a boiled one. A simple omelette (of course, of eggs laid that morning) goes very well beside.

Probably the main reason for growing yellow wax beans is that they are beautiful in the garden, glowing beneath the rich green foliage of the bushes, and beautiful on the plate, as no other vegetable holds so fine a golden color when cooked. The standard among wax beans is still held by the old French heirloom varieties 'Beurre de Rocquencourt,' 'Dorabel,' and 'Roc d'Or,' though the modern cultivar 'Butter Crisp' has its admirers. There are gardeners who grow a few wax beans to mix among green varieties for their added color interest. But as we are always compulsively evaluating all vegetables, and particularly beans, for whatever is unique in them of flavor or texture, we prefer to savor them one variety at a time.

Though fresh beans, when they come in and are of the best quality, are usually to be treated rather simply, Italian flat-podded beans seem to have an affinity for richer sauces and retain their flavor and interest under longer cooking. Also, unlike other bush beans, which we like to leave whole with only the tough stem end snapped off (usually as one picks them, to save a step in the kitchen), flat-podded beans seem best when broken into bite-sized bits. That is a good thing, as it happens, for they are picked a little more mature than other bush beans, and so tend to have strings along either side of the pod, easily removed as they are snapped. 'Roma' has long been the standard among flat-podded beans, and

❧ LEFT: *For sheer productivity, bush beans in many varieties are without compare in the summer garden. They are pretty and compact plants, dark or light green in leaf according to variety, and since they are (like all legumes) capable of using atmospheric nitrogen, they may be planted closely together, hardly more than three inches required between plant and plant. But when the great pole beans come into crop, bush beans should be cleared away as poor relations.*

is an obligatory ingredient in slow-simmered minestrone. For the impatient there is now an improved cultivar, 'Roma II,' which is largely stringless. There is also a yellow form, 'Golden Roma,' which might be nice in a tomato-rich soup, if one found the olive-drab of its parent strain unattractive.

Of all these beans it may be said that they are sturdy, satisfying, abundantly filling, but that among the wealth of summer vegetables, they are not precisely aristocrats. That place is occupied by the true French filet bean, fine both in flavor and in form. With round-podded green beans, or flat-podded 'Romas,' one can slip two or three days in harvest, and still they will be palatable. French filet beans should be picked daily, just when they are half the diameter of a pencil and about five inches long. They are not abundant producers, and so a certain care in presentation is required to make up for lack of mass. They are the sort of vegetable one would expect in a fine restaurant from which one emerged bankrupt and still hungry, as happened once, in Nîmes, when we were served them perfectly formed into a tiny neat bundle on an enormous plate, tied with a bright red ribbon of carrot and resting on an incredibly savory pool of something brown. It is still a possibility in our minds to emulate.

But putting aside the elegance of tiny French filet beans, this truth must be said about all other beans that grow on bushes. Though easy of culture and serviceable in the kitchen, none, in our experience, can hold a candle to the finest pole beans. Pole beans are all true vines, running up to twelve feet if given support. As they require rather warmer soils to germinate, they must be sown more toward the end of bean-sowing time. From first sprouting they will grow like blazes, but the vines must reach a certain maturity before they begin to produce, which is, for us, some-

where around the first week of August. From then until almost the end of September (if frosts are late), whichever pole bean we are growing is the bean of choice, for almost every cooking method and almost every meal.

Like all beans, pole beans are very easy of culture, provided one takes care to give them firm and sturdy support. Without it, they can become a hopeless tangle of vines, obscuring the beans, which, if they are near the ground, will form unattractive brown spots and, like as not, become overmature before they are discovered. We use ten-foot bamboo poles, formed into a tepee of three poles stuck two feet into the ground and tied together with stout bailing twine at the top. Bamboo is slick of surface, and so it is a good idea to twirl a length of coarse twine around each pole, so the vines can cling to it, and not slip down at some point like an overloose stocking on a leg. Three seeds at the base of each pole, nine altogether for a tripod, will quickly build a pyramid of rich green vines, yet another handsome way to vary the predominately ground-level effect of the vegetable garden. Picking, of course, is both easy and satisfying. For once, one can stand upright.

We over-order most things, but pole beans rank with tomatoes as a particularly irresistible indulgence. For anyone below the Mason-Dixon line, loyalty must be maintained toward 'Kentucky Wonder'; we grow it here as well, for its abundant, slender, dark-green pods, superb when about five inches long, but still good when much longer. We are as fond of a pair of old Italian varieties, 'Annelino' in both green and yellow. Like 'Kentucky Wonder,' they are also reasonably heavy bearers, and so similar in flavor that one can mix the green and the yellow into one pot. Recently we have also grown a superb Dutch variety, 'Kwintus,' bred originally as a winter greenhouse producer, but because of its incredible fruit set, a treasure for the summer garden as well. Its pods are long and flat, retain flavor and texture well into maturity, are without strings, and offer, from one tripod, enough good beans for all but the very greedy. Among the beans we grow, it is our current favorite, though as we are as fickle as all other vegetable gardeners, next January's browsing may offer a rival. We'll wait and see.

In our vegetable garden we grow no beans bred specifically for shelling, either to cook fresh or to dry for winter use. That is one of the very few places where a sense of limits controls our activities as gardeners, or indeed in any other way. There is something indisputably wonderful about beans in this class. Their rich names— 'Chevrier,' cannellini, mung, adzuki, 'Yellow Speckle Eye,' 'Vermont Cranberry,' 'Jacob's Cattle,' 'Red Kidney,' pinto, 'Black Turtle'—conjure up cultures as diverse as humanity itself. Shelled or threshed out, they are beautiful, sliding silkily through the hands and, when dried and put up in jars, carrying a sense of well-being, of safety, whatever the winter may bring. They provide a healthful food, particularly when grown in one's own plot, for then one knows exactly what is in them. And, so anciently associated with the survival of our kind as they are, their planting, culture, harvest, threshing, and storing offer a precious connection with the past, a sense of traveling well-trodden paths, without which being human can be a very lonely business. With such a food, it does no good at all to point out that any supermarket, particularly any *gourmet* supermarket, can provide plastic bags of the very choicest sorts, for all purposes, cheaply and conveniently. They may be as nourishing nutritionally, but they are never as nourishing spiritually.

So where is the argument? It has to do, first,

❧ *Like other vining crops such as tomatoes, peas, and cucumbers, pole beans require sturdy supports. To the vegetable gardener intent not only on raising food but also on creating a summer paradise, erecting them is not merely extra work but has an aesthetic component, for the structures created to support pole beans also can offer something fanciful and always handsome, a vertical accent to the horizontal planes of other crops.*

simply with limits of space, for one must grow many rows of beans for drying to matter much, and given the magic of their shapes, colors, tastes, names, and cultural histories, many rows of each. They must be cultivated carefully all summer long before a yield may be expected, and harvest must be timed carefully, on a dry day when most of the pods have formed beans just ready to come loose from their shells, but not so mature as to have cut free already and scattered on the ground. Our part of Vermont tends to be very damp, and so frequently the beans we have harvested for drying were already moldy, though perhaps our timing was amiss, as we know our neighbors bring it off successfully. Perhaps next year we will try again. It is a temptation.

All the beans commonly grown in gardens for table use are New World species with one exception, broad or fava beans, cultivated in the Old World since the Bronze Age, and indeed, anciently preserved from extinction by their importance to the human diet. Unlike their New World cousins, they relish cold, damp soil and the chilly growing conditions that obtain here in late spring and early summer. If, therefore, one does not sow them early, at least by the first week of May, the crop will be a bust, and black aphids, their bane, will move in with the heat of July to finish off a bad beginning. If sown early, however, and in very rich soil, we can count on a moderate harvest by the end of July. There are never very many, certainly never as many as the pounds and pounds we have seen harvested in Greek villages in late spring from a November sowing. And we are so respectful of our plants that we have not dared to pinch out their tender growths for cooked greens, as we know is done wherever they may be grown really well. Our few beans—two or three good servings from two twelve-foot rows—are allowed to reach complete maturity, and then are shelled, steamed on a bed of sautéed onion in as little water as possible, seasoned with bacon fried limp but not crisp (or with good pancetta, if we have been to the city), and served as a first course. That is never enough, but it is very special.

If fava beans are temperamentally adapted to sowing in our cold spring soil, and relish the cool days and nights of late spring and early summer, corn does not. Actually, it grows well here, benefiting from the evenly spaced rainfalls we can count on in most years as a feature of June, and the final arrival, somewhere around the Fourth of July, of what we, high in the mountains, call real heat. Corn is a greedy feeder, so we enrich its seedbed in spring with all the pasture muck we can haul, turning and turning the soil throughout the long spring until it is mellow and fecund. But we must wait until the end of spring for the ground to warm, before the single kernels of seed corn are put in, for they will sooner rot than germinate in the chilly earth. Initially, the corn's growth is slow, though strong roots are put down. With the arrival of settled warmth, it burgeons, almost to the point that one can measure the growth of a single stalk in considerable inches from day to day. Still, we must wait almost to summer's end to harvest, for even in an unusually warm summer it seldom crops before mid-August, and there have been years when we waited until after Labor Day to enjoy what most Americans consider a food more redolent than any other of summer.

But so large are the pleasures of fresh-picked corn that they justify both the wait and the considerable effort needed to produce a crop this far north and at this altitude. The impatient have discovered ways to hasten the growth and ripening of corn, and we have practiced them all. Since the seed is so cold-sensitive, much is gained by starting plants indoors. Like so many other grasses, however, corn is completely unwilling to be transplanted once growth is underway. So peat pots must be used, each sown with two or three kernels, with the heartless plan of snipping out all but the strongest when they reach an inch or two in height. More than almost any other vegetable, corn is the child of light, and few New England houses have windowsills sunny enough to please it. So we use light units, put close to the furnace in the basement, thus providing both light and heat. (The technology of indoor lighting for plants has zoomed ahead in recent years, largely for the benefit of another crop, which might grow well enough outdoors but which is generally best kept from prying eyes. Sources for good light units are to be found in any issue of *High Times*.) But when the infant corn has reached a height of three to five inches, it will want to wiggle its toes in good earth, and the weather may still be too unsettled to expose it to the shock of reality. So when the peat pots are planted firmly in outdoor rows, some protection, either in the form of Walls-O-Water or floating row covers, must be provided. These security blankets can be removed once the nights and days have comfortably warmed, which, for us, is generally some time around the middle of June.

That, however, is not the end of the bother. Corn is a handsome plant, practically from its first emergence until repeated frosts turn it straw-colored and it is gathered into ornamental stocks. Of all vegetable plants, however, it is perhaps the least efficient and the most greedy for space. Each six- or seven-foot-high plant may be expected to yeild at best three edible ears—more likely, two. Considerable room must therefore be allotted for a decent crop in the home garden, and given our relish for it, the most room one has is hardly enough. There is a stupid primitiveness to corn as well, which puts it at the service of no bee or other insect for pollination. Well-formed ears occur only when pollen falls gently from the tassel at the top onto the female silks of the forming cob. So in home gardens, it must always be planted in blocks rather than in single rows, thus wasting as little pollen as possible on wayward winds. Silly as corn is, only thousands of years of human agency have kept it on the earth. Though one occasionally sees "volunteer" plants growing in fields turned to other uses, they are from seed dispersed by the plow, for the heavy ears, once fallen to the ground, rot or become too congested for productivity, or more likely, are hauled away to some small animal's winter nest. No wild progenitor of corn has ever been discovered, and humanity alone is responsible, through glut and famine, for its preservation. Nature, left to her own wisdom, would have dispensed with it some thousands of years ago.

It is well, therefore, that humans like it so much. For if the struggle to grow corn begins with the elements, it very soon devolves to creatures that have brains of their own. The crows come first. They know that each fresh-sprouted grain of corn, pulled from the ground, is starch and salad both, an irresistible meal. We were warned of that when we first came here, and still sowed our corn directly in the rows. "What you got to do," village wisdom cautioned us, "is kill a crow and hang it in the rows. That's a discouragement."

And so we did. Not ourselves, for putting other things aside, we are both very poor shots. A local boy was commissioned, and he duly delivered a handsome bird, quite dead. No crows came that year to molest our seedling corn. But in our second year, we had fallen in love with crows, with their inky elegance in the winter woods, their raucous chatter when snow had muffled all other sounds. So, for love, we became squeamish, and decided to take our chances. Again, no crows came, though by then, as newly transplanted citiers, we had dutifully begun to make our own compost, and perhaps in that there was enough of chicken bones and other kitchen oddments to fill their maws. However it is, we have coexisted with them peacefully from that first ritual murder, and are glad.

Early Summer

❧ Corn is easily the least productive of vegetable garden crops, but a summer without it is a summer missed. Quick and beautiful in its growth, it is to the vegetable plot what hedges are to the ornamental flower garden. Though that matters, it is not of course the point, for of all vegetable crops, corn especially ought to be savored when it has just been picked, hardly five minutes passing between severing it from its material sap and serving it at the table.

We cannot say the same for raccoons. For though village wisdom misled us about the crows, it was dead on target with raccoons. "Better'n you they'll know it's ready. They'll take every ear. Or like as not they'll sample, spoilin' th'rest. They're great samplers." Raccoons are as handsome as crows, and their tiny black hands, their bandit masks, their quiet ways—night folk occupying the garden when we have long since gone to bed—endear them to us. We are glad they are about. But when our first crop was ready, when we went to bed anticipating our first corn on the morrow, the sight of the ravaged blocks next morning—torn this way and that, shredded in the search for ears, none of which was completely eaten, but only wrenched out and nibbled at, tested for the best—created in us an anger we have scarcely ever felt toward any living creature. If we had had a gun, and if they had been there . . .

Like deer, coons can be fought in various unsavory ways. You can spread human hair among the rows, or leave ripe sneakers here and there. You can park the car nearby, or leave a battery-powered radio on all night, blaring the loudest rock station you can find into the quiet woods and your neighbors' bedrooms. Each ear of corn can be liberally sprinkled with cayenne pepper, or, if you are earthy, you can even try urinating in a continuous pattern around the blocks of corn. If fresh blood is in abundant supply, somehow, you can sprinkle it about as well. But when the corn is ready, the coons will come, gross them out how you will. Only one thing works for sure. Electricity. Small units may be bought that run off house current, but as we have electric cow fences near the vegetable garden, we tap from there. Temporary fiberglass poles are inserted at six-foot intervals around the plot, to which three strands of wire are attached at four-inch intervals, to form a charged barrier about a foot high. The coons are kept at bay. But one must remember to step over the fence very carefully when harvesting the corn.

"Why not bypass all this bother," one might ask, "and simply buy fresh corn from a roadside stand?" It is true, certainly, that toward the end of August there are plenty of these stands, springing up it seems at every third house along our rural roads. Corn and other surplus from the garden are offered, always on an honor system, with a cash box to receive change. Sometimes there are also bouquets of simple garden flowers, artlessly arranged in kitchen jars. But though the corn is of good varieties, and well grown, it will have been picked early in the morning (or perhaps the day before) and so will have lost much of its authentic goodness. For as soon as corn is picked, the sugars that give it savor begin to convert to starch. So follows the old country injunction, that the kettle should be at a rolling boil before one goes out the door to pick the corn. Much of the breeding work done with corn over the last twenty years is in response to this fact, and the results are called either sugar-enhanced or supersweet. Of the two, sugar-enhanced varieties (such as 'Sugar Buns' or 'Tuxedo') represent real improvements in flavor, tenderness, and sweetness; unlike with most vegetables, for once the replacements of old heirloom varieties surpass them. With sugar-enhanced varieties, the conversion of sugar to starch is slowed down somewhat, so the ears remain choice even if a few hours elapse between harvest and cooking. The supersweets, on the other hand, are very sweet indeed, and the sugar-to-starch conversion is slowed down (or perhaps simply masked) for days. But at least to us, corn should taste like corn, and candy like candy. The supersweets we have tried are cloyingly sweet, simply too much of a good thing. And so growing your own corn is still the only way to have it at its best, barring proximity to a generous neighbor.

Americans are fondest of the foods of summer. Peas, beans, corn, and tomatoes are most people's first choices among vegetables, regardless of the season. Modern agriculture, modern trucking, and the freezer allow us to have them even in the depths of January. The foods our grandparents ate in winter—beets, carrots, parsnips, turnips, cabbage, and winter squash—were popular then because they kept with little trouble in the cellar all winter long without much loss of flavor; and they were, in any case, sustenance when nothing else was available.

Of course, that required a certain sort of cellar. Old houses in many parts of North America, and certainly in New England, were built over pits excavated in the living earth, the foundations walled up with stones found in the digging or from the clearing of the fields around. Though generally constructed without mortar, these foundations have been surprisingly stable, set as they were into stiff clay subsoils. Such cellars usually have only hard-packed earth for a floor, smooth in dry weather, cool and clammy to bare feet in summer. But they are below the frost line, so water oozes from the walls and trickles across the floor all winter long. And in the thaw of January or in spring's unlocking, rivers are apt to run through. Some of these cellars are still intact after the houses they supported have sunk back into the forest perhaps a hundred years ago. We still find them in our rambles through the woods hereabouts. Strong trees have grown up within their walls, and if the woods have not closed in too tight, there may be a clump of lilacs or perhaps a blueberry bush hovering still near what was once the front door.

Such cellars are hardly pleasant places, hardly the sort of thing a young family of recent prosperity might specify to their architect and their builder as a necessary component of their dream home. Ours is a relatively new house, with a relatively dry poured cement basement, made comfortably warm by the heating unit, the hot water pipes that feed the house, the washer and the dryer. It is a convenient place to store all those things that seem necessary (or not) to maintaining a house—paint cans, tools, the NordicTrack we never seem to use, dry kindling, furniture we mean someday to repair or have reupholstered, all those empty wine bottles. We can even turn it to gardening use, for we have discovered that certain plants of tropical origin—coleus, dahlias, dwarf bananas, and caladiums—will endure a winter with us and burgeon the following spring only in the comfortable heat of such a basement, made light by fluorescent tubes. But like many gardeners, we would have given much for one of those old, clammy, earth-floored basements, spider- and mouse-ridden though they be. There, we might have conducted all sorts of other horticultural experiments—forced spring bulbs, stored sleeping hydrangeas, seen dormant stools of cannas and hedychiums through the winter—and preserved our winter vegetables, beets, carrots, 'Black Spanish' radishes, turnips, parsnips, salsify, and scorzonera, celery packed root and all into cases under a single light bulb, chicory roots in damp peat forcing into witloofs.

Fortunately, for us and for everyone, an alternative to the classic root cellar of antique houses can be contrived. Often, a corner far away from the furnace may be walled or partitioned off and kept at about 40°, with maybe a humidifier added for requisite clamminess. Or one can contrive, as we did, the proverbial "frost-free shed," as in "store in a frost-free shed over winter." Of course, to keep anything frost-free in Vermont

❧ *Cold Storage Shed at North Hill. Though nothing can quite replace the dark, damp root cellars of antique New England homes, a simple shed may be constructed that, with minimal heat, will still keep many harvested crops in good condition throughout the winter. Ours is half of a working cool greenhouse, from which it borrows all the heat it gets. There a whole winter's worth of food is stored, prolonging summer's bounty deep into January.*

requires some contrivance, and so ours, which measures about twenty-five by fourteen feet, is attached to a working greenhouse at the base of the garden. Both shed and greenhouse form one continuous building, sharing both a poured-cement foundation and an inexpensive propane heating unit. Our fuel bill is never very much, since the greenhouse, when the sun is shining, heats both spaces (the greenhouse more, the shed less) and winter temperatures are kept as cool as we dare, which is somewhere around 45° Fahrenheit. The windows of the shed are shuttered in winter to conserve fuel, though light enters through the greenhouse and is supplied additionally by halogen growth units, hung in the ceiling for the benefit of the many tender plants we store—fuschias, buddleias, potted wisterias, citrus trees, hydrangeas, agapanthus, and the like—all of which tend to accept, or require, a semidormancy in winter. Around the darker edges of the shed, conditions are almost ideal for the storage of all the crops we put by for winter use. And though, on a bitter, windy evening when it is time to start supper, we might wish the shed were a little closer to the kitchen, it is never a bad thing to go down and check the greenhouse, admire the tiny species cyclamen in bloom, enjoy the winter fragrance of *Buddleia asiatica* or the early flowers of an orange tree, and pick a sprig or two of fresh rosemary for the potatoes one came for.

All that is far more pleasant than a trip to the supermarket. And a properly stored beet or carrot is, in January, far more interesting on the tongue than green beans harvested last week or the week before in south Florida or Mexico, or January's tomatoes, which neither smell nor taste like summer's bounty, or actually, anything at all. There is, as well, something deeply comforting about a winter larder, connecting us with ancestors who

either provided for their own needs or went without. The question "What shall we have for dinner?" thus becomes not just a matter of pleasant choices among options within close proximity, but also a realization of some vital link, historically and spiritually, with our own past. Finally, there is still something *living* about the vegetables one gathers out of storage. Chicories have actually grown, producing fat witloofs deep beneath a thick layer of peat, signaling their readiness for the table by snouts poking barely into the air. Cabbages and Brussels sprouts are stored with their roots and outer leaves, from which they still draw sustenance throughout the winter. Carrots, beets, and winter radishes, pulled from the damp sand, will display frail white whiskers of root, and may even have produced a tuft of new leaves, not an unacceptable addition to a winter salad. All this, with the smell of life still on it, reminds us, if with a difference, of the pleasures of the summer garden, and of harvesting from a medium closer to life than a plastic bag.

One crop we grow for winter use does not, however, relish the cold, damp conditions of our shed, and that is winter squash and pumpkins. For they are desert plants, and their fruits store best in conditions much more comfortable to humans. We are not sure, with the fifteen or so varieties we attempt each summer, whether we grow them because we like them cooked, or simply because they are so beautiful. We were hooked on them years ago—in fact, in the first summer of our life together and in our first vegetable garden, a modest plot behind a wonderful old farmhouse we rented outside Boston for two years. We were told there had always been a vegetable garden there, though when we came, little remained of it but a splendid thirty-foot border of asparagus, lovingly tended for fifty years or more and still lusty after the few years of neglect it had suffered before we came. In a row along its edge we planted our first winter squash, a magnificent, orange-red Japanese cultivar called 'Red Kuri' with small, minaret-shaped fruits. It scrambled into the asparagus, and hung there, nestling in the blue-green ferns, reminding us of Andrew Marvell's wonderful line describing the oranges of the Bermudas, dangling "like golden suns in a green night." After twenty-eight years, it is the one image of that garden we can most vividly recollect, and an excuse, years after and forever, to grow 'Red Kuri.'

More recently, on a raw and rainy October morning, we visited St. Jean de Beauregard, a chateau just outside Paris that still maintains a magnificent seventeenth-century walled vegetable garden. In a decrepit glasshouse, previously a vinery, all that season's squash and pumpkins had been gathered for curing, a dazzling array of colors and shapes: red, orange, yellow, near black, celadon blue-green, speckled, mottled, striped, oblong, round, squat, mammoth, and tiny. From within the effect was stunning. But it was even more beautiful from without, blurred by the glaucous, ancient glazing washed by rain. We came away that autumn determined to vastly increase our range of these fascinating plants.

Not that we can ever hope to equal that garden. For winter squash and pumpkins are lusty, vining plants, greedy for both rich earth and huge amounts of space. The richness we can easily provide, or more correctly, our cows can, from the residues of their winter feedlot, a fecund mass of seasoned manure churned up with forest earth, autumn leaves, and hay, just the diet that winter squash relish best. Space, however, is another matter. When we designed our present vegetable garden, we fixed its limits firmly with a split-rail locust fence enclosing an eighty-by-sixty-foot rectangle, knowing perhaps that without such defining edges, an image like that one at St. Jean de Beauregard would get us into hopeless trouble. It is true that only the bed in which the seed are planted and the roots develop need be enriched, and the vines may scramble outside the fence, weaving their way among pasture grasses and meadow flowers, an overflowing mass of rich green leaves that only slightly compromises our design. But still we have room for only fifteen or so hills, and so we must limit our choices to that number. That is never easy, for some must be repeated every year, because we like them so much. 'Red Kuri' is an indispensable, not just for the memory but because it is still among the most beautiful of its race, and its manageable size and very sweet, richly colored flesh makes it the first choice for pumpkin pies. The old French heirloom variety 'Rouge vif d'Etampes' is also a constant, its deep ribs, flattened form, and glowing orange skin making it, certainly, the pumpkin that miraculously carried Cinderella to the ball. Caramel-colored butternuts and blue Hubbards are classics in the New England garden, and, with emerald-green acorns, still among the best in flavor. Lately, a white-skinned variety, not, we think, an heirloom, called 'Luna' has become readily available, a wonderful contrast to the colors of all other squash and pumpkins, even if one doesn't want to make of it a ghostly jack-o'-lantern.

After these, we are free to experiment a bit with our choices, selecting always, we confess it, more for unusual form and color than for qualities of flavor. This year we have added a golden Hubbard, a slate-blue Native American cultivar called 'Sibly,' 'Pink Banana,' and 'Silver Bell' among others, all from Jan Blum's wonderful catalog of antique and heirloom vegetables, Seeds Blum, in Boise, Idaho. Added to the varieties we

❧ *All squashes and pumpkins are beautiful in the summer garden and beautiful in their promise of sustenance deep into winter. Here, the Japanese variety 'Red Kuri' twines its lush-leaved vines along the fence, dangling its fruit, first orange and then fire red, as it goes.*

always grow, they should make a wonderful tumble of shapes and colors under the hall table, as many as will fit. We still do long, however, for a decrepit eighteenth-century vinery in which to display our harvest, harder to come by, obviously, than a rainy October morning.

Though the growing of squash and pumpkins has been more or less a constant in our vegetable gardening life, cucumbers have come and gone and come again. In the beginning, we always planted two or three "hills," four-foot-wide beds mounded up a foot or so from the surrounding earth and made rich by compost and well-rotted manure. Why hills are necessary we have never been sure, and each year we have wondered, out of purely scientific curiosity, what the results might be if the seeds were pressed simply into well-dug, level ground. It may be that elevating the beds provides drainage in a wet early summer, for none of the plants that originate in arid places, and indeed few vegetables save celery, will tolerate saturated soils about their roots. It is certainly true that rows and mounds create a structure to the garden from the beginning, satisfying in itself and indicating, before the seeds sprout, where one may safely tread, and where not. In any case, ancient practice indicates the need for molding the earth in this way, and it is so fixed a practice that we have never had the courage to fly in the face of its wisdom. Our hands and shovels will simply not comply.

In the early years of our vegetable gardening, the cucumber vines were simply allowed to sprawl where they would, with no more intervention from us than the occasional bending of a wayward shoot back into the bed. They made handsome ground cover, their large leaves clothing and cooling the summer earth, though it was often hard to locate the cucumbers beneath, and many escaped our notice to become warty, lemon-yellow cases full of seeds. Soon, however, the constrictions of space and our growing interest in making the vegetable garden as beautiful as any other caused us to build all sorts of structures for elevating vegetable vines, annually constructed "follies" fashioned first from maple saplings laboriously harvested from the overcrowded woods, and later of bamboo. There was an especially attractive design for cucumbers, a shorter, six-foot-long version of the tomato supports, an A-frame made of poles threaded with a grid of stout baling twine, like a little house of vines. That made the cucumbers easier to harvest, as they could be spotted dangling within, though as cucumbers tend more to scramble than to climb, each vine had to be trained and tied in, almost daily.

We did all this not so much for the occasional fresh cucumber, which was nice enough but which we ate, rather unimaginatively, just with salt, but to make pickles. In the beginning it was one of our most deeply honored summer rituals. They were in the main not bad pickles, and we remember with particular pleasure a huge crock of kosher dills, from a recipe culled out of the New York Times, seasonal advice on what to do with the cucumber glut. We kept up with it as best we could. But our sense of what a pickle should be was radically changed when we had the good fortune of forming a friendship with our neighbor, Faith Sprague. Her pickles were both humiliating and glorious lessons in what pickles should be, and now that she is ninety-two, they are still as good as they ever were, perhaps even better. The best are "bread-and-butter" sorts, each slice hardly bigger than a dime, pleasantly crunchy, both sweet and pungent, never cloying, actually addictive. From our first taste we have treasured each jar we have been given, and when our friendship with her became a certainty, we gave up the making of pickles, and largely even the growing of cucumbers. We cultivated Faith instead.

Faith and Faith's pickles are still a treasured part of our lives, and will be as promises till she reaches one hundred, and even after, as we have stockpiled many jars, adding to the collection with each visit. So they may be like those heirloom cognacs and brandies one might be served in ancient French farmhouses (or hideously expensive restaurants) hand-labeled "Souvenir de Mme Whatever, 1892," and we will ladle them out in tiny silver inch-high cups. Lately, however, we have returned to the growing of cucumbers, largely through the influence of a new friend, a young Greek student of fashion design named Fotios Bonzikos. He is not much of a gardener, nor a cook either, but an understanding of cucumbers comes to him, as to all Greeks, as practically a birthright. From him we have learned to make a simple but sublime concoction of shredded cucumbers, pressed free of as much juice as possible in a colander, and combined with yogurt and plenty of chopped garlic. Something between a salad and a condiment, it seems

❧ *Cucumbers are always splendid in leaf, flower, and fruit, but never more so than when they display themselves against some support. A fenced vegetable garden provides that, and also makes the harvest of the fruit far easier than when it is concealed by leaves and draggled in the mud. Here, seed stems of the blood-red orach have been left for an early crop of salad next spring, and the cream-colored panicles of the Pee-Gee hydrangea (*Hydrangea paniculata *'Grandiflora') are just forming.*

to go with everything, and be as ubiquitous on a Greek table (and now on ours) as ketchup on an American one. We have learned, too, to make a salad, or rather many salads, no two alike, with cucumbers and sweet onions as a base, with whatever herbs one has—fresh mint from the stream, oregano or thyme from the rock garden, basil, chives, or parsley from among the vegetables—handfuls chopped fine and thrown in. Tomatoes are good when they are in their prime, as are olives, providing they are black, salty, shriveled, and oil-cured in the way of Greece or Provence. Obligatory is a generous crumbling of good feta cheese, and enough virgin olive oil to make everything else in the dish swim in a savory broth laced with enough fresh squeezes of lemon to add the requisite acidity and bite.

The miracle of this dish is that, unlike other salads, it may be left on the drainboard in a bowl to season for a day or two, if it lasts, and other ingredients may be thrown in as they run short. There, it is always convenient for a quick snack, with bread dipped in, or for a gardener's lunch, in which case the bread might be heated in the oven, just to make it seem more like a meal. Endlessly adaptable, the best of such a salad occurs when it has been finished up. Then the remaining shreds of this or that can be strained out and a little more olive oil or balsamic vinegar added to make a rich dressing for a simple green salad of choice lettuces, a memory of things past and an enhancement to what is there.

From a patch of cucumbers it is an odd thing to receive such varied gifts, redolent both of a hundred years or more of New England past (of this past here, on this land) and of the past of another country we have only visited, never lived in, hardly know. From that matrix of enrichment, of borrowing, we could make an argument for cultivating one's own vegetables, if there were not (as indeed there are) so many other arguments to hand. New savors, new ways of preparing and presenting the abundance of the harvest, sometimes even the glut, are always precious. How much more so are they when they link us to friends and to cultures so disparate, though in their love of the land and of good food, they join hands with us. Clearly, we are the beneficiaries of that. Our new interest in cucumbers makes sure of it.

If cucumbers are abundant, peppers and eggplants are among the most problematic crops we grow. Members of *Solanaceae,* the rich nightshade family, which also includes tomatoes and potatoes, they are much more sensitive to cold and wet soils and would be utter failures if seeded directly into the ground. We must make sure, by the time the weather settles in mid-June, that we have lusty, well-grown transplants, preferably already with flower buds on them, and that the places they are to grow have not already been occupied by direct-seeded crops—lettuce or beans or herbs. The soil must be made as rich as possible, and liberally laced with phosphorus, for both crops are greedy for it and without it will produce only a lush crop of leaves. It is certainly a benefit to cover the prepared soil with black plastic, which heats it up, and to transplant directly into evenly spaced holes cut into the plastic. That, however, is a compromise with aesthetics we are unable to make, though when the plants are well established, we are willing to tuck a blanket of hay about their roots, which provides them with some security. In a good, hot

year—one in which the peas stop cropping early, the spinach bolts, and the Chinese cabbages are useless by mid-June—we have abundant crops of both peppers and eggplants, enough for us, who never tire of them, and to give away.

A glut of peppers is always a good thing, for they may be used from the time they have attained a decent size until they are fully mature, well colored and packed with seeds. Happily, they also keep very well when picked, and—we are told—can even be cut into strips or minced and stored in the freezer without blanching with no great loss of flavor. We never have enough for that, even if we were of a mind to do it. The sweet sorts, "bell" peppers to Americans, have so many uses in the kitchen that there is never an excess of them. They may of course be stuffed, with a savory mixture of ground meat, eggs, bread crumbs, herbs, and reduced tomatoes to make a dish that is good hot, and even better cold, in a sandwich or as a first course dribbled with a dressing of olive oil and lemon or balsamic vinegar. Bell peppers may be chopped into almost any egg dish or pasta sauce or Mexican or South American stew, or sliced into ribbons and laid in artful patterns on the right kind of homemade pizza, more crust and vegetables, herbs and good oil than tomato goop and cheese.

We grow pungent peppers as well, 'Habanero,' 'Chipolte,' 'Scots Bonnet,' 'New Mexican,' and the like, and the lethally hot Thai sorts, many of which make beautiful shrubby plants, liberally studded with fruit in purple, red, cream, and ivory, one even with variegated foliage, a surprising anomaly among vegetable plants. These, of course, we treat with care in the kitchen, being sure that they are not overwhelmingly hot in any dish, and that we have washed both our hands and any kitchen implements we use to handle them. We are always glad of a surplus of these to

❧ *Peppers come not only in wonderful shapes and colors, but also in many flavors, sweet, mildly pungent, spicy, or fiery hot. Like folks, each must be dealt with according to what its personality offers, and like folks also, an infinite variety is to be preferred over a bland sameness.*

❧ *Those familiar only with the standard large purple eggplant, pretty in its own way and certainly serviceable, might be surprised at all the other shapes and colors eggplant can come in; for there are cylinders, serpents, bells, and eggs, in black, mauve, purple, vivid orange, or snow white. Though that is the great fun of growing them in variety, and in gathering them, their culinary uses are all pretty much the same, which is to say in dishes requiring a great deal more oil than one ought perhaps to consume.*

string into *ristras* for winter use. We have learned to pierce the stems, and not the flesh of the peppers themselves, which might cause them to rot; to wear latex gloves for the work; and, when the string is quite dry, to give it a night in the freezer so that all lurking bugs are killed. Then, all winter long, a dried pepper can be removed from the *ristra* and crumbled into beans, or plain rice, or the right kind of stew, which should then of course be tasted after a while, when heat has released the pungency, before crumbling in another.

Eggplants are even shyer producers for us than peppers, and that is a pity, for, while almost as versatile in the kitchen, they have the distinction of being able to form the main part of a

meal. We keep experimenting with forms and varieties of eggplant—round, egg-sized and eggshell-colored, long, skinny green Japanese, violet-flecked and streaked sorts of standard size, and of course the most familiar, deep purple-black, perhaps still the most handsome of all. But it seems to be the vagaries of our weather, and not the varieties themselves, that account for an abundance or a dearth of eggplants in the kitchen. We do, however, hedge our bets a bit, for as eggplants are such handsome plants, never more so than when one can see the forming and maturing fruit dangling beneath, we always grow six or so in large clay pots. They ornament the lower part of the garden around the greenhouse, benefiting from the reflected heat of the walls and from the warming of their roots as the sun shines on the pots, and they may receive all the care they need, with frequent fertilizing and spraying of the leaves with the hose to keep down spider mites and aphids, both a bane to them. When early frosts come, the pots may be whisked into the greenhouse, where at least the tiny fruits that have just begun to form will continue to develop, providing at least a few more eggplants for autumn.

Of course, from a dietary point of view, it is maybe a good thing that we never have as many eggplants as we want, for every cook knows that they have an extraordinary affinity for oils and fats. They soak it up like blotter paper, and even when cubed into a soup, they will swim to the top to absorb whatever is floating there. That is the point, of course, of the famous story of the Turkish imam who married a young woman famed both for her beauty and her skill at cooking, and made even more desirable by her dowry, twelve enormous earthen jars of olive oil. On their first night of wedded bliss, the young bride served eggplant, which delighted the imam so much that he ordered it to be served every night thereafter. Things went well for eleven more nights, but on the thirteenth, the eggplant was missing from the table. Furious that he had been disobeyed, he questioned his wife, who replied, "Dear lord, you will have to buy oil for the eggplant, as I have now used up all I brought to you as my dowry." The imam is said to have fainted at this shock, thus the name of the famous Turkish dish of stuffed eggplant, *Imam bayildi,* "the Imam fainted."

There are ways, of course, to cheat eggplant of its craving for fat. It can be soaked in milk, or in meat stock, or in miso broth before it is cooked. The trouble with these methods is that we actually *like* fat in eggplant, which turns it creamy and, in a word, unctuous, making it taste as eggplant should. The most extravagant and still the best way to cook it is to dip slices first in flour, then in beaten egg and then in fine bread crumbs, and plunge them swimming-deep into oil heated to between 325° and 350°. (The hotter the oil, the less of it—relatively—the eggplant will absorb.) We can, however, offer another favorite dish, as good in its own, different, way, and certainly less sinful. It is made by slicing unpeeled eggpants into strips about a half inch thick and placing them peel side up in a shallow earthen casserole in more or less a single layer, tucking between them wedges of ripe tomato, tiny new potatoes if they are in, and chunky squares or broad strips of sweet or mildly hot peppers. A handful of pitted black olives tucked here and there is also nice. The whole dish is then dusted with coarse salt and pepper, chopped parsley, and plenty of fresh rosemary left in sprigs, and then dribbled over with rather more olive oil than one might think healthful, but far, far less than was used by the imam's bride. The casserole is then baked uncovered in a 350° oven until the vegetables are tender, and served hot with roast lamb or chicken, or tepid with good bread as a first course or main meal. Containing as it does all four of the major crops in the family *Solanaceae* grown for food— eggplant, peppers, tomatoes, and potatoes—it is a sort of *Solanum* feast, proving their mutual compatibility as both botanical and culinary cousins.

The trouble to which one is willing to go for something is usually a fair measure of how much it is valued, in the garden as in life. For fresh artichokes we have always gone to a lot of trouble. Before we even thought of growing them in our zone 4 garden, we made a point of bringing home from each winter's trip to California a case

Artichokes are splendidly beautiful garden plants, their four-foot-high fountains of silvery leaves alone justifying their presence in the garden. But of course one wants the 'choke as well, which is the superbly crafted immature bud of their flower. To get it in cold gardens, a very early start from seed in February is required, and the variety 'Imperial Star' should always be chosen.

of tiny, tender baby ones, at that time unavailable in eastern markets. They were succulent enough to eat whole, and so we boiled them to have with butter, marinated them for salad, and baked them with tomatoes and olives, to have at every meal until our supply ran out. But one spring we found a nursery in Pasadena selling year-old plants in gallon cans. At two pieces of carry-on luggage each, we calculated that we could bring home eight if we packed our other stuff really carefully and were restrained in other plant purchases. Transplanted into the garden in late June, they bore abundantly, and we were determined to learn to grow them without having to travel each winter to southern California.

The trouble with artichokes is not actually (as with peppers and eggplants) that they resent our cool summers. In fact, they relish them, making handsome fountains of silver, prickly-toothed leaves. But artichokes are biennials (or sometimes weakly perennial) and require two full growing seasons to form their edible flower buds. Until recently, the only way to get an artichoke to flower in its first year was to play a trick on it, starting the seed in January, growing the plants under lights for a few months, and then chilling them artificially for two or three weeks at 35°, hoping thus to fool them into believing that they had passed their first winter. Sometimes, with this treatment, they will form one bud and perhaps a smaller side bud, and sometimes they refuse to be fooled at all and just grow leaves.

❧ *Pretty as artichokes alone are, one might still have some fun with them by interplanting nasturtiums and even purple basil among their crowns, both of which cohabit nicely with the growing plants and also provide a delicious and attractive garnish for whatever 'chokes one may be lucky enough to bring to the table.*

❧ *Not all the crops for winter use are gathered into the cold storage shed below the garden. Pumpkins and squash, being natives of the southeastern American desert, seem to keep best in conditions comfortable to people. That is a good thing, as they are all very beautiful, and so as many as will fit are tumbled together under the hall table.*

Several years ago, however, Shepherd's Seeds came to the rescue by offering a cultivar called 'Imperial Star' that was willing to give up its bienniality (as some other plants, foxgloves notably, have also been persuaded to do) and set buds the first year. It is not an abundant producer, however, and so, though a single artichoke might be more than one had a right to hope this far north and at this altitude, the at best two it produced per plant were still not enough for us.

So we are moving toward our final solution. Part of this winter's garden dreaming has been to imagine a little house, four feet wide and perhaps fifteen feet long, framed with cedar boards and sided with small-paned barn sash windows.

There will be a long, peaked roof of the same windows, so the structure will stand about four feet high, capable of being opened at the top in hot weather and closed when summer moves to autumn and frosts threaten. With this little house, we hope to extend the productivity of our artichoke plants, and maybe, with thick mulches, to coax them into staying two years with us, producing, or so we devoutly hope, a positive burden of buds. Some discipline will be required to keep other plants out, newly purchased rare shrublings or marginally tender garden perennials. But we are resolved that it will be strictly for artichokes, an artichoke house. Perhaps we are not so far off, after all, from that decrepit vinery.

High Summer

What marks off high summer from the season before is that whereas since June there has been enough to eat, now there is too much. From June onward there has been plenty—lettuces of many sorts, thick rows of spinach, thinnings of chard and beet and the tender terminal shoots of orach (an amiable weed, all about the garden) to add even more variety to the patchwork rows of mesclun. And there have been peas, the tiniest sort, picked early on a dewy morning, the undisputed queen of early summer crops. Turnips have been fine, sweet, and mild, reaching the ideal size that barely fits comfortably between the circle made by thumb and forefinger. Oriental cabbages have achieved, all at once, that brief stage between watery perfection suitable for stir-fry and sodden nastiness, suitable only for the poultry yard. But except for salads, a constant with every meal, and radishes, good anytime between, there is on any specific day in early summer only one best thing to harvest. The rest, though tempting, can wait, and so we go up to the garden already settled in our minds about what will fill the harvest basket.

High summer is different. For now, in mid-July, each evening's harvest poses painful choices. Though we take care to stagger the seeding of the beans, they have all come in together, encouraged all at once by the best growing weather of our season. Summer squash of many shapes and sorts have blown up in the night, obstacles to stumble over in the paths. Peppers and eggplants have gotten down to their essential business and are born to earth by their heavy fruits, too massive it would seem for the fragile plants that nourish them. Potatoes have begun to show their pretty flowers of chloroxed lavender, signaling that tiny, marble-sized tubers might be gently teased from beneath the plants. The fennels, never abundant, are just large enough to justify their harvest, but not so large as to have become stringy and tough, which can happen almost in a night if one waits greedily for bigger bulbs. Two rows of broad beans show enough fat pods to justify picking, and are so precious that they should be eaten by themselves, stewed with onions and bacon, only good bread and olive oil beside, enough for supper. Most prized of all, the tomatoes have begun, shyly, to ripen.

And what is one to do with it all? One solution is to take a significant portion of our daily nourishment in the garden rather than at the table. We graze shamelessly at every opportunity. In the morning, when we go up to tend the chickens, there might be a handful of blueberries or raspberries, fresh from the night's heavy dews. In midmorning, when we return to clear a row of peas, there will still be a few last pods on the vines that are sweet, hardly a noticeable robbing of the cows, who will get the spent vines. A clean, rain-washed lettuce leaf is always nice, or a bit of arugula for a stronger tonic. Rich as we are then, we can also practice various forms of charity, taking baskets of choice produce to neighbors, or tossing to the geese and chickens, thankfully less particular than we, all that is past prime.

But still, we feel guilty that there is so much. For at this season, the whole cast of mind that governs our lives all the rest of the year must be set aside. Rural life, particularly rural life in New England, is an adaptation to scarcity, a willingness to live on the little that can be coaxed from a stony soil in a brief season. But for a few weeks in summer, nature's fecundity overwhelms that reality with the illusion of abundance. And happiness, then, to tell truth, rests just in surrendering to that illusion, in letting go the nearness and calculation that has been, otherwise, the strength of the New England temperament. High summer, like any other happiness, is actually at odds with the facts of our lives. It has, in its long, warm days and pleasant nights, a timelessness and softness, the illusion of another attitude toward living, a grasshopper sense of contentment in which plenitude is the rule rather than the exception.

But happiness too has its disciplines, its proscriptions against greed. How hard it is to pick the smallest beans, thinner by half than a pencil, rather than the larger, thicker pods that would fill the basket in a tenth the time. We know that the tiniest summer squash, still with the half-withered blossom attached, are the ones we should be harvesting, for they bring premium prices in the finest markets, and some part at least of all the labor required by a vegetable garden is the smug circumvention of such extravagances. But a firm, half-formed courgette has a heft to it, a promising, resonant, internal thump that causes us to pause before we throw it to the cows, as we think, "We could grill this, we could slice it for extra juice and flavor into a vegetable soup, we could stuff it, we could look at it, even, in its beautiful perfection of form, on the table for a while." The broccoli is prime, perfect, the dusty green heads, free of cabbage worms, so very broccoli-colored when alive and so dull and nasty a green when they float to the surface in the cooking water. Two or three heads would be good for tonight's dinner, except that we had two last night and the night before. We force ourselves to take a celery from the ordered, military rows, breaking ranks just because a young celery is good to eat while one is waiting for a more substantial dinner, and in any case, what can one do with thirty-six perfectly formed mature celeries in September, wrapped in plastic and burdening the entire lower shelf of the refrigerator? Better to take one now, when it is still small and free of strings, hardly more than three ribs and a tender, butter-colored heart.

So, in this season, we force ourselves to be governed by a certain attitude of thriftlessness, of Lucullian gourmandise, harvesting only the very best and turning away from all that is still good but not at the peak of perfection, or that could have a longer row life to become a burdensome glut in autumn. It is a discipline. And perforce, much goes by. So it is fortunate that while ours are the most particular, they are not the only mouths on our property to feed.

There is, of course, another attitude to take to the bounty of summer, one that we used to practice but have now largely abandoned. Years ago, when we first came to live in the country, we froze much of what the garden produced. We had the time then, for beyond the vegetable garden we had little to tend but a narrow flower patch along the newly planted yew hedge. Most of our present five or so acres of gardens were not even a dream in our heads, though, looking back, we

see that we were clearly headed that way. So each morning we harvested—snatched, almost—everything that the garden offered. We spent whole days shelling, snapping, scraping, and chopping, plunging things into boiling water and then into cold, sealing up plastic bags and packing the freezer. (Pounds of beans and peas and corn; and once—the count has stayed in our heads because of the trauma of it—eighteen large cauliflowers all on the eve of a departure for a vacation.) Certainly there was joy in the process (for we were new to it) and a tremendous comfort in surveying a whole freezer full of the fruits of our labors, preserved and provisioning us for the winter. We walked by the freezer bins of the supermarket with a certain smugness. We contemplated buying a second freezer.

Two things altered our attitude to all these activities. The first was that our interest in horticulture steadily grew, resulting in the addition to our small domain first of a larger collection of perennials, then to a path bordered by antique and shrub roses, then woodland strolls and shade gardens, plantings by the stream, a rock and bog garden down below, a second greenhouse full of tender ornamentals, a collection of rhododendrons and exotic small understory trees, a series of planted walls, a flowering meadow . . . So many days at the stove and kettle meant so many fewer in the garden, and we began to chafe.

Even so, the vegetable garden was hardly displaced in our affections. Though it became a rather peripatetic area, moving to the edge of other horticultural activities as they occurred, we kept it through all this development, never missing a single season; and we kept it as beautiful as we could, out of a conviction, even then, that the usual opposition between the "ornamental" garden and the vegetable garden was false, nothing being more ornamental or of greater beauty to

❦ *When high summer finally arrives, the vegetable garden produces a bounty that will be characteristic of it until a Black Frost comes to cut it down. One hopes for many guests then, not just because the weather is fine and the garden has achieved its peak of beauty, but also to help with the consumption of the produce. Clearly, this tumble of good things is more than two people can get through in a day.*

any property than a well-planned, well-kept area devoted to the raising of food. But tending the neat, even rows, following the exacting routines of seeding, transplanting, harvesting, and reseeding, turning one's back at twilight on perfect order, not a weed in sight and the paths raked, was one thing. It was at least gardening. The canning kettle, the steamy kitchen, and the burdened freezer were quite another. And gardening, suddenly, was all we wanted to do.

The second shift ran even deeper, and was an alteration to our very attitude toward nourishing ourselves. Even in the dead of winter, the products of our labors were good, for we read all the appropriate texts and followed their advice. From the freezer we could choose broccoli or cauliflower, peas or beans or corn, anytime we pleased. In spring, we often had them all together, in orgies of vegetable soups meant to clear the freezer for the next round. Though certainly we were well-fed, and spiritually content at living from our own labors, the broccoli, peas, beans, cauliflower, and corn came to have a certain sameness about them, a predictable ready-on-demand sort of quality that robbed us of much of our joy in them. The seasons were all flattened out, and one sitting to the table came to seem just like another. Worst, we found ourselves making gifts to friends of *frozen* vegetables, which we trust were well received, but which, compared with the baskets of fresh produce they might have been given earlier in the year, were cold and dead . . . frozen, in a word. In desperation, we kept a pig.

Now, both in the abundance of high summer and throughout the year, we live by little festivals, savoring what is available according to the season. We no longer expect to eat everything we grow. Rather, in the plenitude of late July and August we glory in a richness of choice—the mark, the multicolored banner, of that season. There will be

other things later—root crops, cabbages and Brussels sprouts, endives, celeriacs, parsnips, and salsify—that are special in their way also and that will continue to nourish us through the winter until we may harvest the first fresh dandelions of spring. Thus, what we eat connects us directly to the season, brings the table into harmony with the weather outside the windows and with the very ground beneath them. That does not slow down the ever-accelerating passage of time, for nothing can do that. But it does make that passage fuller of meaning, allowing us to mark the progress of our days with fresh peas or beans, a squash or a basket of late, frost-touched spinach, a beet or carrot extracted from cold, damp sand.

Still, no place in one's life is more full of contradictions (perhaps) than how one chooses to eat. So despite our general conviction that the seasons are to be savored as they progress, we make an exception of the fruits with which the late July and early August garden is laden. Jars and jars of strawberry preserves, currant and gooseberry conserve, raspberry jam, apple and blue plum sauce and pears stewed in red wine get prepared and stored ("put up," in the old phrase) in a steady rhythm as high summer progresses to autumn. Perhaps there is no real contradiction there—or, if there is, it is one that aesthetics and not reason must be called upon to resolve. The apparatus required for preserving fruits—the great old unlined copper confiture pan never brought out except at this season, the jars, many of them veterans of seasons of preserving, and all brought from dusty oblivion in the basement to sterilized sparkle—and the process, the way dry sugar liquefies and takes on the colors of the fruit as it heats, the two marrying into a thick, richly colored substance, first grainy and opaque and then tinctured like stained glass, and most of all, the smell of hot sugar and fruit, a smell of pure goodness—all of that is more attractive by far than a roll of zip-lock plastic bags and the freezer. And when the jars are properly sealed and lined up on basement shelves, they convey a sense of something *made,* not merely artificially arrested in its progress toward decay, but transmogrified.

In most cases, the growing of fruit in the home garden is an easy task. Strawberries are perhaps the exception. An established bed can be expected to last only three years at most, after which the original plants become exhausted from bearing and choked with their own progeny, intermatted far too thickly to produce well. Consequently, in early spring, vigorous young plants must be dug from beds nearing the end of their productive life, to be established in newly enriched soil elsewhere in the garden. Well fertilized and kept free of weeds, the new plants may be expected to bear shyly the next summer and abundantly for the following two years. The great trick is to keep leapfrogging the beds, grubbing out old ones just as new ones hit peak perfection, so that the gardener is never left with one exhausted patch and another one too young to bear, a strawberry-less summer. All that is doubtless a lot of work, but strawberry beds, when well tended, are handsome in themselves, a ground cover of thick, glossy tripartite leaves, studded in early summer with flowers like tiny, single white roses (whose cousins they are) and later, as summer progresses, with berries, first green and then the richest scarlet. The fruit, picked at perfect ripeness and full of perfume, is as evocative as anything the garden can yield. Only the surplus gets put away as jam, but it is always enough.

All the currants and gooseberries, however, are put up as conserve. Closely related species in the genus *Ribes,* they are common features in northern and central European gardens and were grown in huge abundance in Colonial American gardens and well into the nineteenth century. Their value in early American kitchens was tremendous, for they are among the hardiest of all cultivated fruits, thriving even into the arctic circle. Though they respond to good culture with increased abundance of fruit, their culture is so easy that they were often left to themselves, to produce as they would at the edges of cultivated fields or vegetable gardens. Their fruits are intensely acidic, so much so that gooseberry juice was often served with fish as an acceptable substitute for lemons. Both gooseberries and currants were pressed when slightly underripe, the juice mixed with molasses and diluted with water for a thirst-quenching summer drink served during haying. Conserves of both fruits were highly valued in winter because of their rich concentrations of vitamin C, easily retained because the high pectin content of the fruit caused it to jell after very little cooking. These conserves were seldom served at breakfast or at tea, but rather were offered as condiments to highly flavored (perhaps overripe) game, and were considered as obligatory as cranberry sauce with Thanksgiving turkey, the only modern survival of the early American preference for sweet, acidic preserves as a side dish to meat. Both fruits could be made into excellent wines and cordials, gooseberries reserved to make a dry white wine sometimes (with luck) as effervescent as champagne, and currants used to make red wines and strong liqueurs, valued as a cure for sore throats and winter colds. Dried currants were (and are still) an important component of steamed puddings and cakes, though the dampness of the New England climate made drying them difficult, and so the imported product was always a preferred luxury.

❦ *When trained into small trees, red currants are both productive and very beautiful. Even if one had no taste for currants, the little trees are decorative in their own right, reminiscent of medieval illustations or antique garden prints. Though the training takes about three years, the resulting standard may be expected to live and produce for fifty years or more.*

Neither gooseberries nor currants are much grown in modern American gardens, though occasionally a few heirloom plants have been carried on, and there are wild bushes, of many antique forms, still flourishing in pasture hedgerows and around the cellar holes of vanished homesteads, where knowledgeable foragers return each year to harvest their fruits. To thoughtful gardeners, it is a source of both fascination and temptation to know that these crops—so easy to grow and so much a feature of lives past, in times of sickness and of merriment—have largely disappeared from our garden culture.

Cultivated gooseberries and currants have disappeared from cultivation chiefly for two reasons. The first cause has perhaps been the power tiller, with its attendant assumption that vegetable gardens are not spaces with features of permanent beauty or value, but rather spaces made anew each year, essentially food factories where efficiency reigns over any aesthetic considerations. The second is that certain species of *Ribes* are alternate hosts of a serious disease, white pine blister rust, that affects the noble American white pine, *Pinus strobus,* and so the planting of all cultivated forms of the genus has been interdicted in many states by law. Gardeners interested in these plants should ascertain from their state departments of agriculture and forestry or from the local office of the Cooperative Extension Service whether and where their culture is prohibited. In fact, it appears to be the black currant, *Ribes nigrum,* is the most active host of the disease, and not the red currant, *Ribes rubrum,* or the white currant, an albino form. Gooseberries also do not appear to be effective hosts for white pine blister rust, and are so abundantly naturalized in the colder parts of the eastern United States and in Canada that forbidding

their culture could hardly make a difference. There is even, for gardeners who can procure it, a host-resistant form of black currant, ambiguously named 'Consort,' that produces a handsome bush to five feet with abundant blackberry-scented fruit, reported to be the best of all currants for eating fresh.

In any case, we have no white pines within five hundred feet of our vegetable garden, which is the maximum distance the disease can travel, and so we grow currants and gooseberries with a reasonably good conscience. They are handsome plants. Left to themselves, they form sprawling, many-stemmed bushes about five feet tall, suitable for a bordering hedge or for inclusion in an old-fashioned hedgerow. But both plants can gain enormous sophistication when trained into "standards," small, mop-headed plants on a single stem, something like what a child will produce when asked to draw a tree. Grown this way, they provide a second tier to the vegetable garden, which is generally otherwise all on a plane, lacking vertical accents. As they are deep-rooted and noninvasive, other crops—beans, cabbages, lettuce, or potatoes—can be planted about their trunks, thus increasing cultivated space. They offer permanent structure to the garden, and in late autumn and winter, when all other crops have been cleared, they are an interesting feature, almost medieval in effect. With other permanent woody plants—espaliered apples and pears, blueberries in rows, and raspberries tied in on wires—they contribute an evocative beauty to a space that would otherwise be dull, merely resting until it could be given interest in early spring by the first green lines of seeded lettuce, beets, turnips, radishes, and spinach.

Of the two species, currants are far easier to form into standards than are gooseberries. One can simply secure vigorous young plants,

establish them in attractive, permanent places, and allow them to develop as they will for two years. Then, in early spring, select the strongest stem and tie it to a stout stake, cutting away all the other growths at ground level. Often, the remaining stem will be as tall as one wishes, five feet or so, but if it is not, all but a single strong growth at the top should be trimmed away, and that growth tied to the supporting stake until it reaches the desired height. Then it can be allowed to bush out into a small tree. No growth at the base of the plant should be allowed to develop, and it is good to follow the advice of the old gardeners whenever unwanted suckers appear at the base of a shrub by yanking them away while they are still tender rather than cutting them with pruning shears.

By the third year after planting, the little tree should have formed a rounded head, dangling thickly with strings of improbably translucent berries, ready by late June or early July for stripping off into a basket (if one can bear to do it) and converting into conserve. Over its long life of fifty years or so, a currant tree will require only the snipping out of stems four years or older, since heaviest fruiting occurs on two- or three-year-old branches, and the trimming back of overlong or wayward shoots that destroy the symmetry of the top. If the plant was established in moist, humus-rich soil, the fertilizer that is left over from the crops growing at its base will suit it fine, though when grown in poor soil or in rows all alone, the trees will benefit from an

annual dressing in early spring of granulated garden fertilizer, 10-10-10 or the like, and a sustaining mulch of organic material—leaves, hay, or whatever is available. So treated, a standard currant may well outlive the gardener who gave it its shape, becoming a small, gnarled tree, still shyly producing in an abandoned garden.

The training of gooseberries into standards follows the same regime, though being spiny, many-stemmed plants of wiry and congested growth, they are slower to develop into small trees, and require rather more snipping and pruning when they are young. One should plan on two, possibly three more years to bring them into perfect form. All the while, however, they will be producing fruit, and so the delayed gratification is more aesthetic than practical. Gardeners who are clever at grafting (which we are not) can take a far easier way to producing gooseberry standards than the patient effort required to prune them straight and tie in a strong, central growth to achieve the desired height. In Europe, gooseberry standards are created by grafting young wood of a desirable variety onto straight rods of one of two native American species, *Ribes aureum* or *Ribes odoratum,* both of which are themselves prized in old-fashioned gardens for their intensely fragrant, clove-scented pale yellow flowers in early spring. As the strictures relax on growing gooseberries in North America, and as more American gardeners become aware of the rewards of their culture, perhaps a source for perfectly formed, grafted standards will become available, or grafted plants will be sent in from Holland, where they are much prized.

But any way they are grown, even as sprawling, spiny bushes, the fruit of gooseberries is wonderful, being translucent, lime-green or rose-tinted fruits shaped like a small egg (hence the botanical name, *uva-crispa,* "crunchy egg"). Even

❧ LEFT: *Our four currant trees produce, at harvest time, a whole canning kettle of fruit. Boiled down with sugar, almost as much currant conserve will be produced as the volume of fruit one started with, to serve with winter breakfasts or after dinner with cheese, or to add, two or three tablespoons, to a sautéed chicken laced with soy sauce and balsamic vinegar.*

the vernacular name, gooseberry, is amusing, fun to say and to think about. As we keep geese, we first checked its etymology in the most direct way, by arranging a neat pile of fruit in the goose yard, just to see. The geese were in fact quite scornful, conveying with their handsome eyes and a dismissive shake of their shoulders that whatever *we* though about that particular treat, it was nothing to them. So we looked into the eleventh edition of the *Encyclopedia Britannica* (1910–11), where we read that the name is probably a corruption of the Dutch *kruisbezie* or the German *krausbeere,* meaning "crinkled berry," though, in a footnote quite typical of that wonderful reference, this fine sentence was offered: "The grounds on which plants and fruits have received names associating them with animals are so commonly inexplicable that the want of appropriateness in the meaning affords no sufficient ground for assuming that the word is an etymological corruption." There is always a pleasure in being left so splendidly in the dark.

But whatever the origin of the name, a bowl of gooseberries is always wonderful, reminiscent of a still-life painting one saw somewhere, once, complete with its perfectly rendered drop of dew or a homely bug carried in accidentally on the fruit. Over the gooseberry's long history of cultivation, varieties have been bred that are more or less palatable when eaten fresh. But most are so acidic that they are better for looking at or for putting up as conserves. Like standard currants, gooseberries seem not at all to mind other crops crowded about their shanks—celery or celeriac or beans or basil—but rather to enjoy it, as a sort of living mulch.

The same cannot be said of blueberries, which are acid-loving plants, shallow-rooted and sensitive to any disturbances around their home ground. The thought of converting one into a

standard has occurred to us, and we may do it someday, if the plant is in the right place and suggests that it is tending that way. In an old Philadelphia garden, we have also seen blueberries trained as a free-form espaliered fence along a narrow strip of ground between pavements. Generally, however, blueberries are so particular in their needs, and so distinguished when allowed to assume their natural form, that we have resisted torturing them into mannered shapes. They are among the handsomest of native deciduous shrubs, so much so that we have planted them as ornamentals throughout the garden, and particularly among rhododendrons, whose cultural preferences they share. For general landscape work, when a small deciduous shrub is needed that will offer interest throughout the year, blueberries are practically the first choice, winning the competition even over fothergillas, viburnums, and enkianthus (all elegant shrubs) without much struggle. It may be said of them that they have everything: ease of culture and freedom from disease, a handsome, multitrunk shape of attractive branches, a moderate stature usually to five feet or so but sometimes, in very old specimens, to ten, magnificent autumn color, delicate (and delicately fragrant) ivory-colored bells of flower in early spring, suitable even for forcing in the dead of winter, and, of course, their fruit.

It is for the fruit that they are planted in the vegetable garden, though even there we appreciate their other qualities. So we have established a hedge of fifteen large plants along the shadier woodland side against the locust fence. It is hard to imagine anything more satisfactory in that place, which does not receive quite enough sun to mature standard vegetable crops. There is huge pleasure in the shapes of the bushes, gnarled and spreading, a perfect visual counterpoise to the

❧ *Though very popular in colonial times, gooseberries now are seldom grown in American gardens. It is a pity, for the fruit is cunning and beautiful, its properties healthful, and a taste for gooseberry conserve or tarts addictive, once acquired.*

horizontal members of the weathered locust fence. Even the berries are beautiful, in modern selections the size almost of marbles, colored to an unusual, rich cobalt blue overspread with a powdery blush. There never seem to be enough of them, in part because birds are as fond of them as are we, one little modest gray bird apparently able to gullet down the produce of a whole bush in a surprisingly short time, putting them all heaven knows where. We used to cover the bushes with cotton net against such depredations, patiently swathing the bushes and securing the ends with clothespins against the wind, unwrapping them each time we wanted to pick and then wrapping them up again. Tedious work, for the season for blueberries is a long one, almost a month. Then,

providentially, we discovered that a flock of guineas (who seem themselves to have no taste for the fruit) discouraged even the boldest feasters, we suppose because guineas look so much like hawks. So for three years we have been able to dispense with netting, and have lost hardly a berry. Things often work in one garden and not another, but are passed on by those for whom they work as infallible wisdom. We would not say so much for this trick, which may not work next year, even for us. And then, guineas being so much what they are, not everyone would want to keep a flock. (Perhaps, if they were a guaranteed deer repellent, even one's neighbors would welcome them.) But for the while, here, it has worked.

Those who love blueberries love them all by themselves, but for a simple summer luncheon dessert, they are both more beautiful and tastier with the addition of a few raspberries in red or gold, and a handful of acidic currants. Of course, a sprinkling of sugar and a generous dollop of whipped cream further improve the dish.

Still, little of what the blueberry bushes offer makes its way to the kitchen, and then only as a beautiful companion to other seasonal fruits, particularly golden and red raspberries, or as a garnish to a lemon ice. Too many years of officiating at pie-eating contests when we taught the eighth grade, watching pretty, blindfolded children, hands tied behind their backs, burying their faces in purple goo to win the prize for their class, seems permanently to have spoiled our taste for blueberry pie or for anything that looks remotely like it. And actually, most of the blueberries we produce are eaten straight from the bush while we work the garden in early morning, or gather

other crops for lunch or dinner. Eaten that way, only raspberries are finer.

And we have an abundance of raspberries, too. Like blueberries (and unlike currants and gooseberries), they profit from being grown in their own place, and not closely interplanted with other crops. So we have established a hedge of them across the back of the garden, one side planted to summer-bearing, red-fruited sorts and the other to amber, late-summer, and fall-bearing ones. With luck, the two will overlap in their fruiting, making possible a compote of red and gold, with a sprinkling of deep blue from the blueberries and the ruby glisten of a few late ripe currants. The result is like eating jewels, a glorious solution to lunch desserts for unexpected guests.

Raspberries are errant growers, and when left to themselves will produce an impenetrable and ever-widening thicket of many interlaced and thorny stems, the oldest of which will never bear but will seem to exist only to catch at one's clothes, bloody one's bare arms, and get in the way of the rich cluster of berries just beyond reach. For that reason alone, it is good to be ruthless in grubbing out any young plant that escapes the row, which is best kept to no more than two feet wide, so that one can harvest both sides easily. Old canes, which may be recognized by their darker bark, must be cut away after they bear to leave room for the new canes, colored a mottled straw. What remains should be tied into wires strung on posts, the first wire at about two feet from the ground and the second at four, to prevent them from arching outward and smothering adjacent crops in other rows. As raspberries are shallow-rooted, it doesn't work to try establishing annual vegetable crops at their bases. Rather, the row should be mulched with leaves, straw, spent hay, or the like, both to prevent weeds and to encourage vigorous growth. As with any other crop (particularly in the Northeast, where soils are deficient in phosphorus and potassium), a light sprinkling of 5-10-10 fertilizer or the like in early spring will encourage heavy fruiting. Though anyone who has an established raspberry patch will have plenty of young plants to give away, it is still good to establish one's own planting with certified, virus-free stock from a reputable nursery, and to be sure that native stands are located far away from the planting, five hundred feet or so, to prevent virus infections.

Raspberries will grow throughout the United States, but gardeners in the southern tier will perhaps have little success with gooseberries, currants, and even blueberries, particularly where the soil is alkaline and summers are dry and hot. But the most cherished fruit of high summer, tomatoes, are grown by every gardener everywhere. And if other fruits grace our table with condiments and pies, ices and jellies, tomatoes will form the heart of every meal we eat throughout August and September.

When we first grew tomatoes, on a rented piece of ground just outside Boston twenty-six years ago, we planted what was available as started plants from local garden centers. They were standard sorts with "big" and "super" in their names, and "boy" and "girl," suggesting in the first instance a country lad bursting his overalls and in the second perhaps something else. By August we had a few ripe fruits of a suitable "tomato red," though most of the crop remained green, and in our ignorance we left it on the vines to become, with the first heavy frosts, gray mush, a thriftless waste. Then, when we came to Vermont to garden, we searched out earlier-ripening, cold-hardy sorts, chiefly from Vesey's Seed on Prince Edward Island, bred to produce in a climate similar to that we had adopted for our life as gardeners. We particularly remember 'Scotia,' which crabbed along the ground without stakes and produced small, ripe tomatoes by the middle of July, good fortune, though the fruit had only a shadow of the richness a vine-ripened tomato should have. By then, however, we had learned something about ripening tomatoes from our canny Vermont neighbors.

What we learned was that half the success of growing and eating good tomatoes well into September and even October lay not just in careful cultivation—in enriching the soil with all the humus available, in starting the seed early under cool, sunny, and buoyant indoor conditions, in planting the sometimes spindly young plants quite deep, two or three leaf nodes below ground, in feeding with a fertilizer weak in nitrogen but high in phosphorus and potassium, in patiently clipping away unproductive side shoots and basal suckers and in faithfully tying in the vines to sturdy supports—but in watching the weather. For even in the hills of Vermont, where insulting frosts come late and early, a crop originating in South America may be expected to produce abundantly in a summer of fine, bright July days and an August that is warm and dry, hot for here. But such summers, good "tomato summers," are rare for Vermont—enough only to be one in three, or four. (Could one but predict them, a sowing of lima beans would be worth the trouble, and the garden, else, might be all tomatoes.) But normally, in our cold zone 4, only a few tomatoes will actually ripen to perfection by August, leaving a great many perfectly formed but still green or slightly colored fruit on the vines. Still, they are hardly waste.

Gardeners, anywhere that winter is a reality, learn quickly to keep alert to frosts. There are chiefly two sorts at season's end. Perhaps as early as the last week of August, light ones may be expected to occur, a mere chilly kiss of what is to come. Those might be called "bedsheet frosts," for that is what one mostly covers the beds with, and if there is not a quantity of old, worn-out sheets put by for the occasion, many a northern gardener might sleep on a bare mattress, and come morning, take a bath rather than a shower, because the shower curtain is on the tomatoes. Half the time, if ground moisture is abundant and protective mists rise up in the night, or if the garden faces south on a slope with good air drainage

(as ours does), the trouble is for nothing. The garden has escaped for one more night, and often several days. Still, covering is always worth the trouble, for one never knows. And generally, the first frosts will be followed by fine, bright, warm days, the glorious suspension of what is certain to come, that perfection of weather called "Indian summer," when tomatoes ripen best.

The other frost has no flirtation in it, but goes about its business with an iron will. It is the killing frost, called Black Frost, occasioned by the first massive sweep of arctic air that is winter itself and from which there is no turning back. Fortunately, when it comes, one always has warning, in weather reports that never speak ambiguously of "the colder valleys," and in the gossip at the local store and post office. ("Black Frost tonight. Better bring things in.") Then, no thickness of bedsheets, shower curtains, old burlap, frayed towels, or salvaged plastic will help. For steadily the earth has lost its warmth, and the bitter air will penetrate through, withering any tender thing to black tatters and certainly making unripe tomatoes not worth the gathering come morning. We always hope that when the definitive warning comes we are at home, well rested and prepared to take pleasure in the final gathering, not only of tomatoes, but of all other tender crops—eggplants, peppers, squashes, and pumpkins—trundling them down to safety in buckets and baskets, glorying in our harvest. There is also a host of frost-intolerant plants that must be gathered in, tender ornamentals in pots, standard rosemaries planted in the ground, the last basil,

RIGHT: *Most of our tomato crop will not ripen on the vine, but rather, in a space at the top of the upstairs hall reserved for them at season's end. This basket contains the immature and partially ripe fruit of a single vine of 'Yellow Pear,' every one of which we would expect to ripen into some usable form.*

delicate salads. But sometimes we have to do it at dusk by flashlight, grim-jawed, proceeding hurriedly from one task to the other, saving by a sort of forced march all the labor of summer. Then we envy gardeners who can put their feet up, sip a glass of wine, and heave a philosophical sigh of relief that one phase of the intense gardening year is over. Envy is a bearable emotion, however, when we know so clearly that what we envy just wouldn't work for us.

Over the years we have become adept at ripening tomatoes off the vine, using tricks passed on to us by our thrifty neighbors and some we have discovered for ourselves. The first is to be sure that all tomatoes brought in for ripening are free of diseases. If at the end of the growing season, vines show withered or yellow leaves at their shanks despite good culture, early or late blight, both soil-borne fungus diseases, have infected them. Both diseases spread from the ground up, and fresh, vigorous foliage may be above the infected leaves, lulling one into a sense of peace, hoping that the plants will grow away from their problem and continue to ripen the promising fruit hanging above the initial infection. Alas, it is not so, for once either fungus has infected a plant, it will spread relentlessly upward, the spores carried on the breeze or more likely by splashing raindrops. Eventually, if the season is long enough, the entire plant will present a denuded look of bare, leafless stems and poorly ripened or rotted fruit, for both diseases affect not only foliage but also immature tomatoes, continuing to multiply after they have been picked. Only novice growers, trying tomatoes for the first time on virgin ground, may be exempt from this problem, which can otherwise be counted on to spoil all one's best efforts at cultivation, however carefully one prepares the soil and waters, fertilizes, and trains the vines.

At the first sign of the disease we spray, holding applications to the bare minimum, which is to say two applications about two weeks apart, using a fungicide especially formulated for tomatoes. It is not a cure, for there is none, but it does arrest the disease, retarding its upward spread and infection of the fruit. It goes without saying, of course, that even limited spraying is an uneasy compromise with conscience, and so should be done as little as possible and with great care. Gardeners who wish to avoid even that careful minimum must face the progressive deterioration of the vines, but not necessarily the spoliation of unripe fruit, often the main part of the crop. Within a day or two of picking unripe tomatoes, they may be washed with a gentle solution of two tablespoons of household bleach to a gallon of water, which will at least discourage the spread of the fungus during ripening.

The second trick is to leave as much stem attached to the tomato as possible, a trick now apparent in fashionable supermarkets, where bunches of two or three tomatoes are sold, temptingly joined together by a green stem. Old gardeners, who must have grown shorter vines than we do, even recommend pulling the whole plant by the roots and hanging it, withering leaves and all, in a dry, frost-free shed. The method makes sense, for the immature tomatoes will continue to draw energy from the vines, and their dangling position will prevent contamination from spoiled fruit lying nearby. But partly because of the varieties we grow, and partly from good culture, we consider a tomato plant something of a failure if it does not reach the top of an eight-foot stake by the end of the season. Interlaced with its neighbors and tied firmly to its support, it is impossible to take as a whole corpse; and besides, no such wonderful thing as the proverbial "frost-free shed" lies conveniently near the garden. So we are content simply to sever the stem of a promising cluster with sharp scissors near the vine, lay it carefully into the basket, and hope that no unripe tomatoes will roll off. That bit of stem does make a difference, for in addition to supplying a little more energy to the fruit, it seals off the top of the tomato, preventing one entry to disease during storage.

Tomatoes ripen best over a long period of time under temperatures that would be considered just slightly uncomfortable by cold-sensitive people, which is to say the temperatures maintained in most old New England houses, somewhere around 55° at night and 70° in the daytime. Dim light is best. Fortunately, we have just such a place, at the top of the upstairs hall where a piece of furniture would be nice, or even a woodpile for the upstairs fireplaces. But it is reserved for tomato ripening, and in its most useful season is covered first with plastic garbage bags to protect the floor, and then with a triple thickness of newspaper as a blotter for the odd rotting tomato, the putrid juice of which would otherwise quickly contaminate its neighbors. There, we spread out the half-ripe and green fruit, taking care, as much as is possible, that no bunches touch. Almost the second day after harvest, perfectly ripe tomatoes can be gathered from the mass, and from then until Thanksgiving, tomatoes of decent quality will continue to ripen, until what remains is hardly worth the bother. It is of course true that flavor diminishes steadily the longer the tomato has been parted from its sustaining vine; but even the last are probably better than any available at that time in the supermarket. Besides, even the last are products of one's own care and thrift, which in itself means something.

In the beginning of the storage process and perhaps for a month thereafter, one is apt to have a glut of tomatoes, actually the peak of the harvest, as fruit that would have ripened in a week under ideal outdoor conditions comes slowly ready. Even those people prepared to live on ripe tomatoes can eat only so many, and so the problem becomes what to do with all the rest. Every cook has recipes for fresh tomatoes, but the one we like best makes even a batch of house-ripened fruit into something special, and can preserve the bounty of summer and autumn well into deep winter and even spring.

To make our recipe, we cull the pile of tomatoes every two or three days, separating out ripe tomatoes and discarding any that show signs of rot. The best, most perfect fruits are piled on an old ironstone platter and put on the table, both as decoration and for eating fresh. Those of good but not the first quality are reserved for oil-baked tomatoes. They are sliced thickly or quartered into an old Mexican pottery bowl bought years ago for pocket change in an outdoor market, glazed on the inside but rough earthenware without, which has become stronger and more beautiful with each use. We handle it with the care appropriate to fine Sèvres porcelain, lest it break, robbing us both of its beauty and its seasonal use. Any other container would do, provided it were not of metal, though of course it is a special joy to prepare foods appropriate to the season in vessels specially reserved for them and mostly put away at other times.

Once our bowl is about two-thirds full, we throw in a great deal of garlic—ten cloves, maybe fifteen, or even twenty if they are small and we are patient enough to peel them, all finely chopped, and two or three splashes more of good olive oil than the most we dare to use, which we have never measured, but suspect to be near a pint. A generous sprinkling of coarse kosher salt is then thrown in along with any lingering fresh

High Summer

ꟼ *Every vegetable gardener collects or creates recipes to deal with the glut of produce a good vegetable garden will (and ought) to offer. Our recipe for oil-baked tomatoes is too good and too obvious to be original with us, but the vast Mexican pottery bowl in which we do it, the steady rhythm of its production imposed on us throughout the autumn, and the results, put by in jars—so delicious, so ubiquitous in meals throughout the winter—make the process, to us, uniquely ours.*

herbs—rosemary, basil, thyme, parsley—and the whole mass is tossed until all the tomatoes are coated with oil. The dish is placed in a slow oven (about 300°) and allowed to bake until the tomatoes have shrunk into themselves and all the flavors are blended into a sum greater than the parts. That will take about two hours, and though one can go about other household business the while, every thirty minutes or so the tomatoes should be pressed down into the bubbling liquid, lest they burn on top. When they are a thick, partially disintegrated mass, the oven can be turned off and they can rest until they can be reheated and processed.

If they *are* processed. For, just as they are, hot or tepid or cold, they may be served from the bowl they were cooked in with nothing more than very good bread to scoop the tomatoes out on and to dip into the tomato- and garlic-rich oil. Served that way, they make a wonderful, peasant-simple first course, or with a good late tossed salad and some olives, a meal in themselves. But as this process forms a steady rhythm to our days from mid-September well into November, we put up most batches, packing the hot tomatoes and oil into sterilized pint jars and sealing them in a hot-water bath for ten minutes at full boil. When cool, the jars are put on basement shelves away from direct light, to preserve their color, to be brought out later, one by one, to make a fine quick sauce for pasta. One jar, turned into a skillet and cooked until it is bubbly and smooth and the oil has separated, is enough for a batch of pasta for the two of us, embellished only with a sprinkling of hard Italian cheese. Two are needed for company, plus the odd jar or so to send away with them if they are suitably impressed.

Recommending varieties of tomatoes is always difficult, for suddenly there are now hundreds of them available, and not all please equally, or perform successfully in the varied climates of North America. We were ignorant of the incredible variety of shapes, forms, colors, and flavors possible in tomatoes until about five years ago, when we were in San Diego installing a garden, and happened on Chino's, perhaps the most famous garden stand in North America. It has been run for three generations by a Japanese-American family, and the rarity and quality of its produce has caused its fame to spread far, even to England and into the pages of *The New Yorker*. At the stand, among perfect little bunches of multi-hued radishes, exquisitely perfumed Chanterais melons the size of oranges, real mesclun (varied, as it should properly be, with twenty separate

❧ *Though one can do many things with green tomatoes, or house-ripened tomatoes, or even (when one must) with tomatoes from the supermarket, the deepest value of a tomato becomes apparent only in a live performance, never in a recording. The contents of this old copper pan, tumbled with its late August harvest and sitting in the cool shade of the grape arbor, require only a knife and a salt shaker to make a meal.*

sorts of greens, all thumb-sized), baby carrots in white, yellow, gold, and red arranged with all the attention appropriate to a floral bouquet, were tomatoes the likes of which we had never seen. There were deeply pleated 'Calabash,' of an almost-black purple; voluptuous 'Striped Germans,' with skins of marbled yellow and red, the blended colors descending to their hearts; tiny 'Yellow Pears' and even tinier 'Currant' tomatoes, in red and yellow, hardly the size of a pea; and, most remarkable of all to us, there were 'Red Peach' and 'Yellow Peach' tomatoes, about the size of a Ping-Pong ball, furred on the outside with down and firm and flavorful within. We bought them all, enough to savor, and enough, as well, to save for seed. For if one is going to go to all the trouble required to grow tomatoes of quality in southern Vermont, one might as well grow varieties of ancient lineage, gorgeously varied in their colors and shapes, and worthy, come tomato-eating time, of something like a *dégustation de tomates*.

It was worth the trouble. To begin with, even so short a time as five or six years ago the offerings of most major seed companies and most garden centers were limited to standard varieties, reliable in their ripening and uniform of quality, but often sadly deficient in flavor and certainly deficient in a sense of history and in the joyful pleasure of gathering a harvest diverse in shapes, colors, and sizes. A few good gardeners, mostly considered committed cranks, knew how to search through abstruse catalogs and heritage seed banks—or to save seed of varieties grown by grandmother or passed on to them by other gardeners. For the most part, however, gardeners were content to plant what was recommended by major catalogs or buy started plants of whatever sort from local nurseries when tomato-planting time came around. In the main, the results were

good, assuming good culture; but the pleasure was a shadow of what it might have been.

Recently, however, there has been a sort of revolution in the attitude most home gardeners hold toward tomatoes, and to all other vegetables grown in the home plot. Like all really useful revolutions, it has started both from the top and the bottom, from horticulturists with aristocratic credentials and from simple dirt gardeners who remember the old way of doing things and continue to do them according to the way they learned. The result has been a return to home gardens of wonderful heirloom varieties, not only of tomatoes but also of all other crops, particularly potatoes, beans, and members of the squash and pumpkin group. Now it is possible to find tomatoes like 'Pruden's Purple,' 'Purple Calabash,' 'Mortgage Lifter,' 'Yellow Peach' and 'Red Peach,' and the like in many seed catalogs. But it is still worth saving seed of particularly good forms of tomatoes from year to year. We learned this the hard way. One year, having so much to do in the garden (and noting that one of our favorite peach sorts discovered at Chino's was offered by a good seed house), we neglected to save our own seed. What we grew that year from bought seed was not what we had grown before. Though the first tomatoes looked the same, on closer examination we saw that they lacked the fuzz, as if someone had given them a shave, and much of the taste of the previous season's. Where Chino's peach tomatoes had been both sweet and pleasantly acidic, these were sweet and bland. Clearly, not all 'Yellow Peach' tomatoes were equal, and we were sorry not to have carried on our original seed.

We subsequently learned that open-pollinated seed, as opposed to hybrids that are all genetically identical, can vary considerably from one plant to another. 'Red Brandywine,' for example, is praised by many as being among the very best tomato in flavor, but it has been a disappointment to others, causing them to wonder what all the noise was about. There are at least two 'Yellow Pears' in circulation, one of rampant growth and abundant production, with shiny, inch-long elongated fruit born in the manner of cherry tomatoes, many to a truss, and with indoor-ripening and storage capacities equaled by no other tomato that we know. The other is (or has been for us) a hesitant bearer, with three or four fruits to the truss, each about the size of a hen's egg and somewhat pleated, picturesque certainly, but hollow inside, mealy in texture, and of poor flavor. And the elusive 'Paul Robeson,' bred in Russia, where the great athlete and actor-singer lived for years, is in its best form a purple so deep that it is nearly black. But it is among the most willing of cross-pollinators, and so anyone lucky enough to secure that form should certainly save seed, and even, perhaps, grow the next generation far from other varieties. There is, of course, little reason to save seed of any tomato that has not pleased, though there may well be reason to try another batch of seed offered under the same name, particularly when other gardeners rave about it and have it to swap. When any tomato does particularly well in one's own garden, however, and has memorable qualities, first of flavor and then of shape and color, seed should be preserved for planting the following year.

It is very easy to do, but it requires some special tricks. One cannot simply spread the seed out onto a plate or bowl, for the gelatinous material surrounding the seed will cause them to stick as they dry and make them impossible to pry loose without damage. When large quantities of seed are to be saved, they must be scooped out and freed of pulp by soaking them in water for two or three days until the pulp has slightly putrified

and sunk to the bottom. The seed can then be strained out, rinsed several times, and drained in a sieve, when it can then be spread on a slick surface such as a piece of window glass or a highly glazed porcelain bowl, until it is thoroughly dry and can (with luck) be scraped loose for storage. That process will be necessary if one intends to plant a whole acre of some particular variety, or wishes a large quantity of seed for trading with other gardeners.

Because of the vast number of interesting tomato varieties, however, and the space limits of most home gardens, only a few viable seeds of any form will be needed. In that case one can employ another process, amusing in its obviousness and simplicity. Seed can be pressed out onto a single sheet of paper towel and nudged around until they are in a single row, each seed spaced about half an inch from the next. The paper will become quite damp from the pulp it absorbs, and so should be left spread out or even hung up in a cool, airy place until it dries. Then the name of the variety is written at the top of the sheet, which is rolled up into a tube, secured with a rubber band, and put away in a dry, dark, cool but frost-free place until spring. Come tomato-sowing time (eight to ten weeks before the last frost-free day in one's area), the paper towel is unrolled, placed entire on a seed flat filled with sandy, free-draining, humus-y compost, and covered with about an eighth inch of the same material. Watered well and kept moist, the seed should germinate within a week or two. When the tiny plants have formed their second set of true leaves, they should be transplanted into single pots of similar soil, well watered, and grown in a sunny windowsill or cool greenhouse, or under fluorescent lights. Temperature conditions of 50° to 55° degrees at night and 10° higher in the daytime will produce sturdy, stocky plants ideal for transplanting into the garden when all danger of frost is past.

With either method, the tomatoes chosen for seed should be exactly the ones that look best to eat—perfectly formed and colored, true to the desired type, and blemish-free when ripe. They should be ones nearest to the ground, one or at most two trusses up on the stem, where the greatest number of mature seeds will have formed. Those selected for seed should be allowed to remain on the vine until past ripe and on the way to spoiling, which requires both a certain discipline in the gardener and a firm admonition to weekend guests, whose sense of helpful garden labor often extends no further than helping to harvest. Only when "dead" ripe should the seed tomatoes be picked, brought in, split open, and processed for sowing their seeds the following year. It is of course a sacrifice of present gratification for future gain. But in addition to securing tomatoes true to variety, superior in flavor, and fascinating in varied forms and colors, saving seed provides as well a sense of continuity in the garden from year to year and a certain sense of pride, if not of positive smugness. ("You haven't liked 'Pruden's Purple'? Oh well, you should try *my* form of it.")

Despite the fact that special varieties of tomato have been bred for specific climates, we have found that most of the antique and heirloom sorts we have tried in Vermont produce creditable to abundant crops of fruit, particularly if one goes to the trouble of ripening them indoors. They are, after all, survivors over many generations, and as most originated before the development of the trucking industry and the supermarket, they are far more suitable to the home garden and the market stand than to agribusiness and the packing industry. Like any other tomato, they may be expected to thrive in any reasonably good garden soil, but they appreciate extra humus, dug in deep, since their roots may penetrate as much as five feet into hospitable earth, and the even moisture they require is ensured by spongy, humus-rich soil. Unless very well rotted, however, animal manures, particularly horse or poultry, should be avoided, both because an excess of nitrogen will produce lush vine growth at the expense of fruit, and because tomatoes are unusually susceptible to "burning" from fresh manure. Dryness at any time can produce one of two problems or both: "blossom-end rot," recognized by blackened and rotted areas at the ends of otherwise sound fruit, and cracking, caused when abundant rain follows a drought. Regular deep watering is therefore necessary in most areas of the country, though care should be taken never to splash the foliage of tomatoes with water, which may spread fungus disease. The best way to water tomatoes is the tedious method of turning the hose on at a mere trickle and leaving it at the base of a plant, remembering to move it to the next after an hour or so. (If one *does* remember "after an hour or so," for most gardeners have started up suddenly from the dinner table, or waked in the dead of night, fumbling for the flashlight, remembering that they didn't remember.) One can hardly overwater tomatoes if the soil in which they grow is well laced with humus and is free-draining. But any spot where water stands in puddles for an hour or more after watering or a rainfall is sure to be fatal, for they are intolerant of "wet feet."

Full sunlight, as much as is shining, is obligatory, and only heartache and failure will result from attempting to compromise with this most exacting need of tomatoes. Even an hour or two less sun caused by morning or evening shadows cast by trees, tall shrubs, or buildings can retard the formation of fruit by a week or two. This makes the southern end of our vegetable garden, which at high summer lies in cool morning shadow until ten o'clock, unsuitable for growing tomatoes, though the high maple and beech trees that surround the meadow in which the garden is located happily form what gardeners call a "heat trap," guaranteeing greater success at the eastern end than we might otherwise have. (Fortunately, there are many other crops—blueberries, celery, celeriac, spinach, radicchio, and other salads— that relish those cool shady mornings and grow perfectly at the shadier end.) Also, our garden lies at the highest point of our property, perhaps a hundred feet above the house and two hundred above the shaded rhododendron glen at the lowest point of the property. So sun comes early there and lingers late, and cold night air drains away, nice for us and also for the tomatoes, as appreciative as we of the extra hours of brightness and warmth that are there.

Such luck obviates the need to search out most tricks and devices for securing a reliable and early crop of tomatoes. Not so for others, however. We have neighbors whose gardens lie low and trap the cold, who have had great success with small, easily dismantled greenhouses of aluminum tubing covered with a plastic skin. Set directly on the ground, they are enough to provide the extra heat the tomatoes need early in the season to form, though still they must be located in the brightest spot of the garden. As these structures are enclosed and free of wind when the first blossoms appear, the gardener himself must be the pollinator, by vigorously shaking the plants with his hands each day, or by contriving, as a local market gardener we know has done, a "jiggler" made from a massage vibrator and a tuning fork. In this way, he has vine-ripened tomatoes of fine quality as early as the Fourth of July, even in Vermont.

As one cannot have home-grown, vine-ripened tomatoes too early, perhaps someday we will come round ourselves to some such temporary structure in the vegetable garden, though generally we are hostile to any synthetic structures, vegetable gardens being by nature such old-fashioned places. But maybe we have made the first step already by accepting the use of Walls-O-Waters, plastic cylinders pleated into tubes that are filled with water as a nighttime protection against late frosts. Their use allows us to transplant young tomatoes into the garden a full two weeks or more before it would be safe to do so otherwise, thereby gaining that much ripening time later in the season. The young plants grow away like blazes under their homely shelter, seeming much more vigorous from the first than those planted later without them. Still these walls are maddening devices, for water is, after all, a sloshy sort of thing, and the plastic is flimsy, and so they can collapse in a brisk spring wind, crushing the infant plant and proving impossible to set right once they are down. Fortunately (though one is seldom told it in the catalogs that sell them), the solution to the problem is quite simple. When they are first filled with water and put into place, three slender bamboo plant stakes should be inserted into the ground within, making a tepee to form a supporting frame. That way, they are at least stable, though hardly good-looking, and we are always relieved when the weather settles and they can be cleared from the garden.

As soon as they are gone, we replace them with a far more handsome structure, the support system for the vines, which as a piece of temporary architecture gives us pleasure from the moment it goes up. It is made of ten-foot bamboo poles; two feet are stuck into the ground, leaving eight feet for the vines to clamber up. We plant tomatoes in two parallel rows about four feet from each other, spacing the plants about two and a half feet apart in the rows. Two poles are stuck at an angle next to each plant, and where they cross above, the two are tied together. When all the poles have been put in place, a ridgepole is rested across the top within the Y formed by each two poles and tied in for greater stability. Though the resulting structure seems light and delicate, it is strong enough to withstand the most violent summer rainstorms and to support the considerable weight of the vines.

When neatly done, the structure provides the pleasure of an attractive vertical accent in the vegetable garden, which is apt otherwise to be rather boringly all on one plane. (Much more fanciful structures could of course be created—pergolas, towers, stick castles—unloosing the sort of creative whimsy usually reserved only for scarecrows.) Supports for tomatoes are necessary, to prevent the vines from sprawling across the paths, to assist ripening by exposing the fruits to sunlight and air, to minimize damage from slugs and other insects, and to make the work of removing unproductive side growths easier. Virtually all heirloom tomatoes are "indeterminate," which is to say that the vines never stop growing, continuing to extend at the top and to produce side growths along the stem and suckers at the base, until frost puts an end to their efforts. In their natural world, they are adapted to several means of reproduction: the vines root wherever they touch ground, and the fruit ripens and germinates within the colony or is dispersed by animals feeding on it; being actually tender perennials, they can regenerate from rootstocks where frosts are not heavy. Of course it hardly matters to the tomato how it reproduces, but as fruit is the aim of the gardener, and not thickets

of lusty, ever-expanding growth, it will matter to him or her.

All indeterminate tomatoes will need therefore to be tied up off the ground, and most will require the removal of suckers and side growths as soon as these can be pinched out with thumb and forefinger, for it is doubtful, in cooler climates at least, that any but the very first side growths will produce usable fruit, but certain that all the rest will suck energy from the vine at the expense of early, well-ripened tomatoes of decent size. So as soon as the young plant is tall enough to be bent to the stake, it is tied in, or looped in loosely, rather, for one must always take care that the ties are not so tight as to constrict and strangle the stem as it expands. Old gardeners favored strips of bedsheet or nylon stockings for tying, but as the first are glaringly white or colored, and the second are so redolent of other things, we use organic twine, either salvaged from haly bales or bought in a huge spool from the hardware store. (Wire or plastic must be avoided, as when tying up any plant, since both can act as a knife, cutting through tender stems as they expand or move in the breeze.) With twenty or more vines to tend, it is a good idea to cut a generous bunch of eight-inch ties over morning coffee before the work begins, thereby avoiding the distractions of perpetual unwinding, measuring, searching for the dropped scissors, and snipping as one goes. Tomatoes grow with astounding vigor throughout late June and July, and so the work of removing side growths and tying in the vines should be done every two or three days, or at least once a week.

In the main, it is pleasant work, a little repetitive, though on a fine, sunny afternoon one can fall into a sort of rhythmic trance over it, and the results are, when done, a little like administering a good spelling lesson in the fourth grade and having the papers all corrected. Each vine has its own personality, both by genetic makeup and by the thousand variables that cause a living thing to grow one way or another. Generally, when a vine has already formed one or two trusses of fruit, one does not risk saving and tying in a promising side growth, even when it already shows a stem of pale yellow, upturned stars of bloom. But if the main shoot and a side shoot are about equal in development, it could be risked. Sometimes, too, a sucker will have developed at the base of a plant that is full of vigor and shows a promising beard of white rootlets at ground level, too lusty to discard over one's shoulder. So the work of pruning and tying in must be interrupted to find a place for it, where another vine has failed or just in a bare spot against the fence. Established early in the season, planted deep (two or three nodes above the rooted portion), and kept moist until it "catches," it might bear decent fruit. Small-fruited tomatoes, often with other fruits in their names (as "cherry," "currant," "pear," and "peach") and some modern hybrids, such as 'Sweet One Hundred,' bear so prolifically, even on secondary growths, that all strong suckers may be tied in, the vines pruned only enough to keep them in reasonable bounds. Some small-fruited tomatoes are descended from *Lycopersicum pimpinellifolium,* the currant tomato (as opposed to the other wild progenitor of domestic tomatoes, *L. esculentum*), and these are apt to be the ones that come up in northern gardens at the edge of the compost heap; as they bear abundantly and store well, it is always worth plugging such a plant into a gap.

Thus one moves through the tomato rows, making judgments according to either knowledge or instinct, or that uncertain combination of the two that is, after all, good gardening. Unlike some other chores, even in the garden, each pass through gives one a sense of what has worked, what hasn't, what might have. And at the end of the chore—if it can be called that—one's hands smell of tomato, a signature fragrance of full summer, not sweet or piney or herbish, but unique to itself; and when those hands are washed, the water will run green, as good an explanation as can perhaps be achieved for the expression "green thumb."

Sometimes, as we work the tomato rows or sow crops or prick out some rare plant meant for another part of the garden, we modestly wonder how all the knowledge we have of the vegetable world came into our heads and, more mysteriously, into our hands, thumbs, and fingertips. In our sense of what we know, the word "modestly" figures large, and is not put in here as a polite courtesy to those who may know less or a protective concession to those who surely know more. Rather, it reflects our sense of the realms we have yet to learn about, all of which are waiting for us, if only our appetites, our circumstances, our capacities, and our lives last out the possibilities.

Which of the four will go first? We doubt it will be circumstances, though relatively trivial events in life have a way of turning things round, and someday one or both of us may say, as Lillian Hellman did when she contemplated her years with Dashiell Hammett on a farm in Wisconsin, "I once knew how to do so many things . . ." Appetite, for knowledge of how things grow and new knowledge still, ought to remain constant, or even "grow the more by feeding," but our relationship, intertwined now over so many years, might cause one of us to sicken in appetite, were the other removed. Capacities, both physical and

❦ *By the end of high summer, antique varieties of tomatoes ought to have reached the full height of the bamboo structures that support them. Though rich with fruit, both ripe and unripe, these vines still show a bareness at their shanks, the unmistakable sign of fungus diseases, held at bay but never conquered. Still, there are, and will be, tomatoes enough.*

mental, prove unpredictable with advancing age, though gardeners, at least in our partial observation, seem to fare better there than most people. Still, we will have to take our chances, and be fairly determined. As for life itself, the very greatest plantsmen we have known, Linc Foster and Marshal Olbrich, are now both dead, and we who learned so much from them can hardly guess at the fathoms of knowledge that lay beneath what we were able to absorb. But the knowledge is there still, in books, in conversation, even, as one works it, in a row of tomatoes.

$\mathcal{A}$utumn

$\mathcal{N}$ow is the beginning of our longest season. Not by the calendar, of course, for autumn—like spring, summer, and winter—measures three months and has, by calendar date, its own clear beginning and end. We judge otherwise, however; for its beginning, so slow and sleepy, hardly differs from late summer except that fruit ripens, crops are ready to pull in, and frost, if it comes at all, comes first in a sort of brief kiss, leaving us to flirt a little longer with the previous season and anticipate yet the season to come, like partners alternating in the slow patterns of a dance. So much of early autumn is summer itself, or rather, summer brought to fullness and fruition. In the flower garden, the abundance of asters and the exuberance of tropicals—cannas in full sail, dahlias burdened with their improbable flowers, morning glories shingled over each morning with blue—seem to have waited until just now to show what they are meant for. In the vegetable garden

❧ *No gardener needs the first turning of autumn leaves as a warning against imminent frost. Then, all that is still usable in the garden must be gathered in save the hardiest crops, and the autumn discipline of clearing the rows, covering them over with compost, and turning them up in preparation for spring, still so far away, must begin.*

the splendid autumn crops—waxed cabbages in red and green, flags of leeks, bitter green puntarelle, towers of Brussels sprouts—still shoulder the tender crops: ripening tomatoes, peppers, eggplants, late beans.

Shortly after the great blaze of foliage turns the air itself to orange, enough frost comes to warn us that the tenderest things must be brought in, leaving only the hardiest plants to sweeten with the progressive alterations of frost and still mild weather. Though the garden is still rich with produce, it begins to look a little lonely, less inhabited, as rows where tender crops stood become bare, having been turned over and composted for spring sowing. Their produce is piled in halls and odd corners of the house, heaps of tomatoes ripe and ripening, pumpkins and squash in balanced pyramids, peppers and egg-plants in baskets standing about the kitchen, waiting to be stored or transformed into some-thing else. Fruit is everywhere, not the soft lus-ciousness of strawberries and blueberries or the sharply acid, shiny globes of currants and goose-berries but rather the durable and solid shapes of pears and apples, which we can store. Clusters of Concord grapes, watched eagerly throughout early autumn, tested with mouth-puckering results, are finally ready to eat, their fragrance telling us more reliably than any tentative taste that they are ripe. The house now smells as the garden did, though richer and more concentrated from the trapped air, and the garden smells sharp and pungent, scented by frost-withered broccoli, autumn leaves, and cow muck.

A few weeks later, generally in mid-October but earlier if the weather is unseasonable, hard frost comes, killing frost that in one night turns the corn gray where it still stands, and warns us that the second-to-the-last sequence of crops must be brought in. We harvest now with frozen fingers, digging leeks that may have the firmness of ice within them (but will be the better for it when they thaw) and beets and carrots that wear little collars of gray-white icy dirt at their necks, adding weight to the buckets. Last broccoli must be taken then, too, but if we are lazy, Brussels sprouts and cabbages might stand a week longer, not more, until they are pulled as whole plants, root, earth, and all, and piled in an odiferous mass in the cool shed of the lower greenhouse. Cox's Orange Pippin apples must be pulled, even gath-ered from beneath the trees if the mice have not been at them, and they are sherbetlike in the cold when we stop to sample one. Then, in November, snow comes, and winter comes, almost always to stay.

There was a time in both our lives when we missed all this, or caught it only in brief snatches. We were schoolteachers, and the end of summer was the end of gardening, at least of the sort of gardening we have practiced since we ceased teaching. Teaching was a passion too, carrying its own time-consuming labors, its own drains on the spirit, and its own endless, trivial tasks. When summer ended, we were elsewhere, both actually and in our minds. We were in school during the steadily shortening days, and mentally we were there in the evenings as well, organizing lessons, marking papers, figuring grades, rereading clas-sic English texts we felt we almost knew by heart, just in the hope of finding some fresh way to hook country kids into a love of such things. Our autumns were then only weekends and twi-light dashes out into the chilly evenings to toss squash into a blanket and strip last tomatoes from the vines. Too often (though we must still hope we did some good there) we were at parent con-ferences or PTA suppers or endless faculty meet-ings as the sharpening chill increased and we missed our chance at the garden.

Having time at one's own command is perhaps the greatest luxury any human being can enjoy. Most people wait for it until the end of their working lives; too often, then, the special savor of it is brief or already lost entirely. We were very lucky, and we remember our first autumn of freedom (the first, actually, since we were four years old), when time stretched before us, at our disposal entirely according to whim or need. Every night seemed like Friday night. Of course we worked hard, harder in a way, in a different way, than we ever had before. But the long, long season that autumn actually is unfolded for us as it never had before. For that reason, perhaps, or just because it is what it is when one is free to enjoy it, autumn has remained our favorite season of all in the year. To those who have a garden, and care about the table, each season offers its own causes for celebration, its own little festivals; but in autumn they become concentrated, each day it seems presenting its own ripeness. By late autumn, the whole year has reached a crescendo of plenitude.

Of all autumn crops, none grow better here than the brassica clan, variously represented by broccoli, cauliflower, cabbage, Brussels sprouts, kale, and kohlrabi, and each year by curious new entries such as 'Romanesco' broccoli—as much cauliflower as broccoli—and by the anciently cultivated broccoli rabe, the bitter taste of which, once acquired, is forever craved. Botanically minded gardeners—or those who simply like to read up on things—will find in the clan some fascinating information. For all their diversity of growing habits and shapes and culinary uses, they are not separate species but rather all forms of one species. Botanists seem to agree that the original progenitor of all garden brassicas was *Brassica oleracea,* a lowly, foot-high plant that grew wild on the seacoasts along both sides of the English Channel. Our earliest documentation on its cultivation exists in Roman texts, though the Romans, great lovers of vegetables that they were who took what they found wherever they found it, were not the first to raise it for food. That distinction belongs to the Celts, and so it is not for naught that cabbages have become so associated with the Irish.

It is impossible to say at what point the original plant, growing about a foot high, with smooth, shiny leaves and loose heads, began its diversification into the many forms we now know. In appearance, its closest modern descendent appears to be the plant called Portugal cabbage, or *couve tronchuda,* seldom grown in American gardens except in the Portuguese communities around Providence, New Bedford, and Cape Cod. It resembles something like a cross between a very poorly grown, stalky cabbage and a broccoli, though its stems, leaves, and loosely folded heads are delicious, and are an essential component of many Portuguese soups and stews. But if *couve tronchuda* were the only entry in the chapter on cultivated brassicas, it would be just one more oddity in the garden, grown half as a curiosity and half for an occasional good dish or two. In fact, however, the development of *Brassica oleracea* spreads out like a fantastic fan, encompassing many forms that, though recognizable as belonging to the same species, take on incredibly varied shapes and characteristics. For all their diversity, though, the flowers, seed pods, and seeds show no appreciable difference from one variety to another, and so crosses are possible that could produce garden-worthy plants of other shapes, and probably will.

In its most familiar forms—cabbage, cauliflower, and Brussels sprouts—*Brassica oleracea* has long been a staple of the Anglo-Irish diet, joined by broccoli when it began to be popular after World War II. The one of us who grew up near Philadelphia with an English grandfather and an Irish grandmother can hardly remember a meal in which one of these vegetables was not served. Generally, however, for those who liked them, there was never enough, for they were served more as a condiment to meat and potatoes than as a sustaining food in their own right. Three Brussels sprouts to a person was the general rule, though there was always plenty of cole slaw, because it was "better the day after."

There, however, our culinary histories divide, for in the Louisiana childhood of the other of us, okra, butter beans, field peas, and fried corn were far more apt to be served. Cabbage occurred occasionally and collards often in winter, but the former was cooked to a pale-green mush, and the latter, to a slimy, dark-green mass. Either would of course be boiled with a slab of salt pork to season it, and the main part of the dish, it seemed, was that pork, chopped into bits and floating on the greasy cooking liquid ("pot likker"). A wedge of fresh cornbread, liberally buttered, was an obligatory accompaniment.

Until the American culinary revolution that occurred in the sixties, it is probable that most brassicas were mistreated in American kitchens. A slightly crunchy cauliflower or an emerald-green Brussels sprout would have been sent back to the stove. In Fannie Merritt Farmer's *Original Boston Cooking School Cook Book* (1896), for example, only Brussels sprouts, cabbage, and cauliflower are mentioned; one is told to boil Brussels sprouts for twenty minutes (and serve with white sauce), to boil cabbage up to one hour (with a pinch of baking soda, to prevent odors), and to cook cauliflower "until soft" and serve it, again, with white sauce, hollandaise, or cheese. Irma S. Rombauer, in *The Joy of Cooking,* attempts, as one

would suppose, to reverse these practices: "The old way of cooking cabbage is to cut it in sections and boil it for hours. The new way is to shred it finely or quarter it and barely cook it—allowing only 7 minutes if shredded, 15 if quartered." She treats Brussels sprouts, cauliflower, and broccoli with equal respect, preferring brief steaming to boiling, and even recommending, in the case of broccoli, the use of poaching paper "to retain excellent color." In her repertory, of course, are also fine rich sauces, of cream and cheese and eggs, to make brassicas go down better for those whose childhood memories gave ample instruction in how to loathe them and push them quietly to the side of the plate. But cooked properly—lightly steamed to the point that a knife blade inserted into the stem end penetrates only with some pressure, buttered a little (if one must), and sprinkled with salt and fresh pepper, all the homely brassicas can justify their place on the table, and might indeed, in season, make a decent lunch all by themselves.

That having been acknowledged, we must perhaps note here our favorite way of cooking cabbage, though we do it at most once a year, and we have skipped a year or two along the way since we were first introduced to the method. More than twenty years ago, at the venerable restaurant in London called Simpson's on the Strand, we ordered (as one must) roast beef and Yorkshire pudding. It came with cabbage, a whole head that had been wrapped in a clean napkin and steamed in a colander over simmering water in a large kettle for eight hours. Eight. The waiter was very clear about that, and allowed that it admitted of no compromise. (We have since found that six will do, if one is in a terrible hurry.) The results were smooth and buttery, almost of spreading consistency, and one could never have called the cabbage overcooked (as in so many childhood memories of abused cabbages); rather, it had become transmogrified into some other substance. In that, though a lowly vegetable, it perhaps resembles other things people have learned to relish—aged beef looking like the grave, lambs that have passed the stage of mere sheep to the sublimity of mutton, pheasants hung until their heads part from their bodies by sheer gravity, medlars that are never palatable (if at all) until they are quite rotten.

However it was, we vowed to do it. But anyone who tries this method with a head of cabbage should be warned that at some point—around the middle of the day—there is a horrible smell in the kitchen (and most everyplace else), something like a water-treatment plant. In our first attempt at the dish (process, rather) twenty-five years ago, we were living in a very proper rented apartment on Boston's Beacon Street, opposite the Public Garden. Around noon, the landlord knocked at the door and said very politely, "Excuse me for bothering you. But *have* you taken out your garbage lately?" That smell goes away after a while, but one must remain vigilant while going about other tasks, making sure that the inch or so of water in the bottom of the kettle does not boil away, for then everything will be ruined—kettle, cabbage, and all. There may be some electrified device with a timer that could start the whole process in the dead of night, knocking one queasy with one's morning coffee but getting the job done just in time for midday Christmas dinner. Lacking such a device, however, one must simply put the cabbage on first thing, and if timing is a little off, it can cook for an extra hour, more or less. At that point it would hardly matter.

We should mention one other way of cooking brassicas—in this case cauliflower—not because we have ever done it, but simply because we have savored it in memory for many years.

Somewhere in the copious and wonderful writings of M. F. K. Fisher is an account of the cold-water flat she inhabited in Dijon with her first husband, Al Fisher, when he was a student at the university there. Both were cheerfully impoverished, very young, and very much in love. There was only, as we remember the tale, a bed-sitting room and a tiny kitchen, with a two-burner gas stove and an oven of sorts. On it, and on a very tight budget, Fisher was responsible for feeding her husband, and also any friends he brought along from his classes, as he was prone to do. One dish was a sure success, and our memory of her memory of it is so splendid that we have never (yet) tried to do it. The dish started with one perfect cauliflower from the street market, or perhaps two. Taken home, it was broken up into rather large florets, which were evenly dispersed across the bottom of a shallow earthenware baking dish, the sort of common pottery, we imagine, that is glazed inside but is bare clay without. Among the florets were tucked cubes of Gruyere cheese, as much as one had money to buy. The casserole was then filled with heavy cream almost to its top, and baked until the cream and cheese were bubbly and the cauliflower was quite tender. It was then brought straight from the oven, put in the middle of the table, and those who were there to dine dipped in, mopping good French bread directly into the rich sauce. A simple dry, thin white wine, served very cold from the windowsill, was all else that was needed to complete the feast.

Scholars of the work of M. F. K. Fisher could tell us precisely where this passage lies, and they would certainly correct us on our facts, which we have chosen to let remain only in memory. (Were there bread crumbs across the top, dotted with butter, to form a crust? Could there have been bits of ham, which might have been nice but which might merely have compromised the purity of the dish? Would a slight brush of nutmeg, hardly a pinch, have enriched all the other tastes? Was it white wine that was served, or would it rather have been a sharp, thin red, drawn into the bottle at market from a large plastic cask?) Details hardly matter. What matters is that once some people dined very well on the simplest ingredients, simply prepared, and one of them left behind a memory of it, which we in our turn remember. One dines best anyway, perhaps, in memory. When we met M. F. K. Fisher she was very old, dying of Parkinson's disease, hardly more than a beautiful skeleton, living on warm milk with some gin in it. But she had all those memories to feast on, simple dishes such as this and incredibly complex ones, the finest galantines, the most elaborate truffled chickens in chaud-froid sauce, garnished with poached coxcombs. So, until her death, she remained very well fed. We'll try her cauliflower some day, when the mood is right, enhancing or disturbing memory with the facts of direct experience. We hope it will be—as she was fond of saying—"very good."

But though these two recipes are dependent on attentive cooking, the first gaining its suaveté simply from time, and the other from rich ingredients that become almost (not quite) the main thing, generally all members of the brassica clan are best treated, at least on a day-to-day basis, very quickly and simply. Still, it is doubtful that they will give all they have been born to give, unless they have been properly grown. For despite their diversity of forms, all brassicas retain a genetic similarity, and thus, a memory of the conditions of their native place. Originally, *Brassica oleracea* throve on the deep-soiled, mineral-rich cliffs bordering the English Channel, where nights in summer are cool, and where

abundant moisture, in the air and in the ground, kept their large leaves and stems turgid, free-growing, and tender, and where sharp weather sweetened them in autumn.

All that is to say, not California, where most brassicas available in the supermarket are now grown, and where what the lack of what they like is compensated for by artificial irrigation of desert soils, frequent spraying against pests and diseases, and copious amounts of chemically produced fertilizer. They may be harvested at any season, given a little chilling either in refrigerated warehouses or on the road to cancel out their sharpness, as they travel by truck and railway car from the Central Valley to markets in the Midwest, East, and South. Thus, one can have Brussels sprouts (if one wants them) at any time of the year, even in July. But anyone who has only eaten Brussels sprouts "fresh" from the supermarket (even in their proper season), all arranged carefully in their little plastic tubs, will find them at once sour and leathery, no matter how carefully they are cooked. Nothing about them indicates how splendid a vegetable they can be, after frost falls and they are snapped off, one by one, from the trunk of the parent plant, each one crisp and icy in the cold twilight harvest.

There may be places in North America where brassicas grow better than in Vermont, but still they grow very well here, so much so that in the nineteenth century, cabbages, cauliflower, Brussels sprouts, and kale were a significant part of the economy of our state. Then, approximately only 10 percent of its land was wooded, chiefly those parts that were so rocky and steeply ledged that all other uses of it were impossible. The remaining 90 percent was given over to truck farming, dairy farming, and raising sheep. From such activities Vermont had a thriving agricultural economy, capable of supporting many families since departed, their sturdy dwellings now sunk to stone-lined cellar holes buried in the woods. For, given the hilly terrain, holdings were perforce small, not measured in thousands of acres but in hundreds, two or three at the most, and fields were smaller still, forty acres or twenty-five or ten, wherever fertile land had been carved by glaciers between steep slopes and gorges. Our landscape, so familiar to us now with its miles of dense woods, would have looked quite strange all open fields, where soils were deep planted to cabbages, carrots, or rutabagas, and where they were thin and rocky given over to pasture that supported flocks of sheep or stolid cows.

There is no significant truck farming now in Vermont, because the development, first, of the western rail system in the early part of the century and, later, the trucking industry made the cultivation of small fields by single families and "hired men" impractical, especially as land could only be worked four months out of the year. Sheep disappeared as well, because their winter management made the production of wool, lamb, and mutton economically unfeasible, first in competition with western ranches of vast extent, and then with New Zealand. Steadily, the land reforested itself, to the extent that now 90 percent of it is wooded. Dairy farms are still a profitable enterprise, and the roughly 10 percent of land now open is largely given over to them. That provides a pleasant rural character, to the delight of tourists, and—thanks largely to Ben and Jerry—an emblem for the state, whereby Vermont is suggested by anything (a bus, a mailbox, a saltshaker) painted white with irregular black markings suggesting the hide of a Holstein cow. We hardly doubt that the collapse of Vermont's agricultural economy has made a very much more beautiful landscape, whatever damage it has actually done, along with the collapse of similar economies in other eastern states, to American culture.

But it is still true that many people who choose to live in rural Vermont do so in part because they can have a vegetable garden. Not every vegetable can be grown well here—or, at least, not without effort, and not better than elsewhere. But brassicas thrive, delighting in our open, neutral to slightly acid soils, our cool nights in summer, our abundant and evenly spaced rainfall throughout the growing season. Most crucially, the frost patterns in autumn occur gently at first, enough to put an end to tender crops, but just enough to add depth and complexity to the tastes of the hardier brassicas, broccoli at first, then cabbages, and then Brussels sprouts and kale, which may even be harvested from beneath early snows. Their culture here is very easy. All they ask is a rich, sweet soil, which we attain by annual applications of cow muck and copious liming. Those brassicas grown for their edible flower buds—broccoli, cauliflower, 'Romanesco' broccoli, and broccoli rabe—must be grown on steadily without a check from occasional drought, and so, though we cannot water our vegetable garden, we make sure that there is extra water-retentive humus in their soil, and if drought threatens around the Fourth of July (it will not occur here at any other time), we mulch the plants heavily with spoiled hay or partially decomposed leaves from the woods.

Here in Vermont, brassicas have only two pests, though both can be quite devastating. The first is the cabbage worm, the caterpillar of a small white moth that flutters quite prettily around plantings of brassicas in warm weather. The caterpillars are cunning things, their presence in the garden made known by shredded leaves and by thick deposits of digested cabbage

❧ *Members of the brassica clan—cabbage, cauliflower, Brussels sprouts, kale, and the like—are among the hardiest of garden crops and, indeed, are best when slight frosts have fallen on them. In addition to improving their flavor, frost burnishes their beautiful colors, as with this late-seeded red cabbage, destined to be cooked with a little sugar and a splash of sherry and red wine vinegar, in the Danish fashion.*

parts; but if not by that, by the fact that when a head of broccoli is steamed in the kitchen, the caterpillars, which before were exactly the color of the leaves and florets, turn a sick olive green and stud the broccoli throughout in their various stages of existence from tiny, maggotlike things to fully developed worms the size of a piece of macaroni. Unless one's eyesight is very good and one is paying attention, it is very easy to go through the whole process of steaming broccoli, cabbage, or cauliflower before realizing that it has had other, less appetizing seasonings than butter, salt, and pepper.

Fortunately, however, there is an easy cure for cabbage moths. There is a bacteria which, when ingested by the larvae at any stage, destroys their digestive systems. It is a strain of bacillus first isolated at the University of Thüringen (and thus is called *Bacillus thuringensis,* or simply B.T.). Sprayed in dilute form on the plants when the moths first appear, and again two weeks later, it completely eliminates cabbage worms, but it is harmless to all other forms of life, including other insects, and so may be used with safety. Happily, also, there is another strain of bacillus, B.T. 'San Diego,' which has the same effect on the dreadful potato beetle.

The other common plague of brassicas is far less easy to deal with, and far more heartbreaking. Where brassicas are grown on the same ground year after year, they are subject to a disease called club root. The first signs of trouble are when perfectly thrifty-seeming plants suddenly wilt in the midday heat. Pulling one up will show a knotted, congested mass of root, more a series of white swellings than anything one could call a healthy root at all. The disease is caused by a soil-borne fungus and is most apt to appear in soils where acidity is far below neutral, pH 7.0. There is no cure for plants once they have become infected. Much worse, when the fungus has once established itself in a soil, it will affect not only all members of the cabbage group cultivated for their leaves, stems, flowers, or offshoots, but also those cultivated for their roots, specifically turnips and rutabagas. Other important vegetable crops within the family *Cruciferae* may also be affected, among them radishes, nasturtiums, and cress. Even ornamental members of the mustard family can carry and succumb to the disease, such as sweet alyssum, lunaria, hesperis, *Crambe cordifolia,* and many rock-garden plants, such as drabas, iberis, arabis, and aurinias.

Rotation of crops is usually recommended as a practical preventative, for this and other pernicious diseases of vegetables. How practical that may be in a small garden, or even a sizable one in which large numbers of the cabbage family are grown, is doubtful. One must simply do the best one can, remembering that even cruciferous weeds, such as pepper grass, wild mustard, or Saint Barbara's weed, can support and spread the disease. More efficacious a preventative than rotation is an annual test of the acidity of the vegetable garden, and applications of enough lime to raise it to neutral, pH 7.0. That takes a surprising lot of lime, but the alternative is not at all acceptable. It is a sensible caution, as well, to examine the roots of all brassicas bought as started plants from nurseries, and to pass them over if they show any suspicious swellings or white nodes.

Brussels sprouts and cabbage are among the most serviceable of late-autumn crops, holding in good condition a long time in the garden, a month or more after they reach maturity. Both also store extremely well, either in the refrigerator or—as we prefer to do it—simply by pulling whole plants, roots, outer leaves and all, and piling them in the cool shed of the lower greenhouse, where humidity is high and where night temperatures are kept as close to 40° as we can manage. With a covering of moist burlap and an occasional sprinkle with water, both may be taken in good condition well into the winter. Brussels sprouts seldom last that long, because we are very fond of them as a late-autumn and early-winter vegetable; but we have harvested cabbages deep into winter and even early spring, extracting still-firm heads from beneath an odiferous and rather revolting, but protective, slime of leaves. It is worth noting, however, that cabbages store best when they have not quite reached full maturity, and certainly before the heads have split. Therefore, they are best sown a little later in spring than one is actually able to

do, perhaps after an early crop of spinach or radishes has been cleared away.

Broccoli and cauliflower are far more fragile, both in the amount of really heavy frost they can endure and in their storage capacities, which, unless they are frozen, are virtually nil. The problem is compounded by the fact that a whole row of either is apt to reach maturity at close to the same time. With broccoli that is not a dire problem, for after the first central head is cut away (and it had better be, even if one had broccoli the night before, even if there is no one to give fresh broccoli to), flavorful side shoots will develop, and an individual plant can be kept in reasonable production for a month or so. Once the pretty, small yellow flowers that signal complete maturity of the

❧ *Cauliflower varieties now exist whose leaves fold over the curd, keeping it white and saving the gardener the work of patiently tying the inner leaves together. We do not aim for huge heads, preferring those just large enough for a meal for two. Unlike broccoli, cauliflowers will never produce more than one tight, bunched inflorescence, and so the outer leaves are a special treat for the chickens or the cows.*

plant have developed, however, its life is over, and it will not make fresh florets of quality under any treatment. Here we should note, however, that those who are fond of batter-fried vegetables or tempuras might let a few broccoli florets develop past the tight, green stage that is considered most desirable for other cooking. Some overmature florets are apt to develop anyway, by accident if not by intent, but the looser form holds batter more evenly and the florets fry more delicately in hot oil. Even almost mature flower heads may be treated this way, with lovely results.

With a cauliflower, however, once a head has developed—whether it is the size of a child's fist or as big as a soccer ball—that is all the plant has to give. No side shoots will ever develop. So it must be harvested at prime, and that may often mean that the kitchen is flooded with cauliflower. (Once, on the very eve of a week-long trip, we realized that our whole crop was ready at once, all eighteen plants, probably the largest and finest cauliflower crop we had ever grown.) Of course, cauliflower freezes easily and the results are good. But if that is not an option, the only other is a sort of cauliflower delivery throughout the town, to all one's neighbors. Fortunately, some years ago, Vesey's Seed in Nova Scotia offered an obvious solution to this problem, both with broccoli and cauliflower. They developed "all-season" blends, composed of several varieties with different maturation dates. So now we plant both broccoli and cauliflower, expecting that a

❧ *Romanesco broccoli, which seems to be half broccoli, half cauliflower, is merely one more of the genetically identical selections made from an anciently cultivated plant,* Brassica oleracea. *Though now common in supermarkets, it was new to American gardeners as recently as five years ago, causing one to wonder what, after two thousand years of cultivation, this clan may still have in store.*

few plants at a time will mature over a period of a month or more.

Those seedings give us our main crop of both broccoli and cauliflower. But we continue to experiment with other varieties not included in the blends. We are very enthusiastic about 'Romanesco' broccoli, with its beautiful chartreuse minarets perched atop three-foot stems. It is actually, in appearance and in kitchen uses, much closer to a cauliflower than a broccoli, and one might think that it is a cross between two species rather than what it is, simply an intermediate phase between two plants of genetic identity, all three grouped under the botanical designation *Brassica oleracea*, botritis group. Be that as it may, it is a wonderful addition to the brassica clan, with a sweet flavor and a mealy texture unlike any other brassica.

And finally among brassicas are collards and kale, which share the common parentage of all other brassicas, but are grouped by botanists under the heading of *Brassica oleracea*, acephala group. Both are unusually handsome plants in the garden, in all their varieties, and they differ from one another more in hardiness than in individual characteristics or culinary uses. Collards are fairly tender plants, grown from a spring seeding for autumn harvest, though they are never any good until they have experienced considerable cold, and even a touch of frost. In the South, in zone 8, they can become almost perennial, standing in fields or gardens throughout the winter and providing useful harvests in the form of individual leaves stripped from the plant, from the time cold weather sets in (cold for there) until spring. Kale, by contrast, is the hardiest of all the brassicas, so much so that an old New England variety, now so far as we know no longer available, was called 'The Hungry Gap,' for its capacity to stand in good condition throughout winter,

providing greens rich in vitamins long after other leaf vegetables had been consumed in autumn, and before wild herbs—dandelions, Saint Barbara's weed, marsh marigolds, and the like—could be gathered. We love the appearance of both plants in the garden, particularly kale, smooth or puckered, in various shades of glaucous green to purple. It, at least, is very easy for us to grow, developing quickly from an early-summer seeding to form handsome plants when practically all else in the garden has been stripped away and the rows are bare.

For anyone eager to eat what the seasons offer and to harvest fresh crops from the garden for as long as the seasons allow, kale is a very valuable crop. Those who are really devoted to it look at all other brassicas as a pale second choice. But the trouble with kale, for us, is that we have never come much to like the taste, at least when it is treated simply, steamed as one would a Brussels sprout or a floret of cauliflower or a wedge of cabbage. It seems at once too sweet and too slimy. (There are in fact old English recipes that treated it as the central component of a dessert tart, enriched with eggs and spices and honey.) Our best success with kale has been to cook it in the Italian manner, first by frying many cloves of garlic in plenty of good olive oil, then mashing them with two or three anchovy fillets when they are lightly browned and soft, and adding the kale all in a mass, turning it until it is limp and tender in the hot oil. If one has perhaps some white beans from a previous meal, and a few links of sausage, fried and cut into rounds, they can be thrown in at the end for a very satisfying dish. But of course, many other things may be cooked in that manner, and some—such as broccoli rabe, the leafy tops of Brussels sprout stalks, very mature radicchio, or the slightly bitter heads of smooth escarole—seem better, to us at least.

❧ *As is true of corn and many other garden crops, there is no comparison between freshly dug potatoes and their supermarket counterparts. This fine hill of potatoes shows signs of scab, a disease that most often occurs in overrich, manured soil. Still, so fragile are the skins of the potatoes at this stage that it is easily scrubbed off, in no way impairing the flavor or the texture of the potato itself.*

❧ *Potato plants are generally grown from pieces of last year's tubers, called "sets," and so each vine is a genetically identical cutting of the parent stock. This has made the preservation of ancient and heirloom varieties of potatoes possible, so that the gardener may have a choice of hundreds of varieties, all true to form, each offering special cooking and flavor qualities.*

We neglected to say that in this rough-and-ready recipe, a few tiny potatoes, boiled until just tender with the skins left on, are a nice addition as well. That brings us to the subject of potatoes, which of all the crops we grow are perhaps the most important, followed in versatility only by tomatoes, their near cousin in the important Solanaceae family. We have always grown potatoes, for as long as we have gardened, and their history with us is the history of our various vegetable gardens, in many places, and an explanation, perhaps, of why we grow vegetables at all. That question was settled for us, more than twenty years ago, when we were gardening on rented property and struggling to maintain a garden far too large while also accustoming ourselves to the regimes of teaching in small country schools, new to us then, and very exhausting. A friend stopped by and offered what he hoped was good counsel.

"Why don't you at least give up growing potatoes? You can buy a fifty-pound bag for ten dollars in the farmers' market. They'll be as good as yours, like as not, and you'll save yourself a deal of work."

It takes, sometimes, just that sort of foolish but well-meant advice to cause one to acknowledge one's true loves. At that time, as we remember, we were growing only common potato varieties—'Katahdin' and 'Kennebec' and 'Burbank Russet.' It was twilight, cold for June, and we were just preparing the rows for planting. But standing there, we could imagine the intense pleasure of bringing in the crop, the crisp early-autumn Saturday morning, the first plunge of the fork into the hill, the lift away from the earth, and the scattering about of wealth, twenty and sometimes thirty potatoes to a hill if the weather had been kind and we had done the work of growing carefully. There is perhaps no harvesting pleasure

equal to that of bringing in the potatoes. Gathered into bushels, smelling of themselves and the cold earth one should leave about them if they are to cure well, spreading them about on the floor of the dark cellar, they remind gardeners that they are not so far, in soul at least, from countless generations of providing ancestors. ("The crop is good. The winter is secure. One can rest.") Then there is the pleasure of cutting into a fresh raw potato, crisp as a cucumber with a sound no store-bought thing can equal. And the dish or two of the tiniest new potatoes, hardly as large as marbles and carefully sifted from the cold soil at digging time, not one lost. Give up the growing of potatoes? We never could. We would grow them in an apartment window box if we had to.

Far from following our friend's advice, over twenty years of gardening we have vastly expanded our range. 'Katahdin,' 'Kennebec,' and 'Burbank Russet' are gone (though they might return, for we miss their sturdy, stolid reliability). They have been replaced by choicer forms, 'Lady Finger,' 'Yellow Finn,' 'Urgenta,' and 'Peruvian Purple,' and each year the list grows of those we have experimented with, and discarded, not because they didn't live up to their claims, but simply because there were so many others to try. It is ironic that the world at large—or at least the world of gourmet specialty food shops, however extensive it may be—has come in the last ten years to share this enthusiasm. Though it is still true that few select potatoes can be bought in a fifty-pound bag in the farmer's market, one does now find 'Yukon Gold' routinely offered in supermarkets (for its claims are not to be ignored), and other unusual varieties are now to be found with fair frequency in the specialty markets of large cities that cater to people who really care about their food. Still, we grow our own potatoes, and always will. For no other crop adds so much character to the vegetable garden, to the table, and to the joy we take in bringing in our own produce. It is true, too, that we can get something else, something better, from our own potatoes, even when the same sorts are available in markets.

One would think that there is not much to say about so basic a thing as a potato. Handmaiden to countless steaks, ubiquitous inclusion in billions of family meals, solitary sustenance of the very poor, and the essential cause (by way of the Great Potato Famine of 1846) of so rich a tincture of Irish blood in America's veins, its entry into the Old World is something of a mystery. "To the Spanish," the great eleventh edition of the *Encyclopedia Britannica* (1910) firmly states, "we owe this delectable esculent." However, it seems probable that Sir Walter Raleigh first introduced the potato from South America into North America, and that from there it made its way to England. (If this is the case, for the good the potato has done, Raleigh might be forgiven his unquestioned introduction of tobacco, the potato's near relative.) But however the potato came, one wonders in what form it came. Was there just one sturdy, blocky white one, something like what later came to be known as the 'Idaho Baker'? Or would it have been something like 'Peruvian Purple,' or the long-preserved 'Cow Horn'? Maybe a whole bundle of genetic possibilities arrived, multicolored as a basket of

❧ *Varieties of potatoes have come and gone in our garden, some for general use, some for salads, and some frankly for their odd colors and shapes. 'Lady Finger' is one that remains, because of the quality of its waxy yellow flesh, which holds together under most cooking methods, and because its flavorful, thin yellow skin need never be peeled away.*

Easter eggs, later to be crossed and recrossed into the bewildering range of shapes and colors now available.

It is an odd thing to say about so sturdy, so redoubtable, a thing as a potato, that it has had a reevaluation, even a renaissance. But it is true, for the genetic diversity of the common potato, though perhaps not now as vast as it was when most every farm had its own varieties, ready to trade, is still far greater than those gardeners who assume that a potato is just as potato might realize. Although all domestic potatoes appear to have descended from one wild progenitor, *Solanum tuberosum,* their genetic pool is extremely rich. Each tuber is essentially a cutting of the parent plant, true to variety and easy to carry over, making it possible for home gardeners to preserve distinct varieties for many generations. Thus the range of potatoes available is very great, even among other heirloom vegetables that have been carefully preserved, and that exist in a plenitude of shapes and forms far beyond the offerings of run-of-the-mill seed catalogs or the local supermarket. It is, in fact, hard to number the potato varieties available, and each year seems to offer more, each with its own curious name and its own claims in the kitchen. At present, we would guess that catalogs that offer specialty and heirloom vegetables might list, collectively, as many as a hundred varieties, many of which— once one knows their names or even is simply arrested by their curious shapes—might also be found in gourmet markets in winter, ready for planting in spring.

Gardeners should be forewarned, however, that many potatoes offered in markets have been treated with a chemical that retards sprouting. We have no idea what this substance is, or how it works, but we do know that a potato so treated will never sprout, or will sprout too late in the season to produce a crop. Any tuber that produces fat white shoots in storage, or even in bins in the kitchen while waiting for use, will produce a mature crop of potatoes if planted in the garden in spring. But potatoes purchased from the market that show no growth close to planting time had better be tested before planting. Each tuber should be washed in cool sudsy water, using any standard dishwashing liquid. The tubers should then be rinsed in cold water and buried in barely damp peat or sand and kept in an environment comfortable to people, around 70°. After two or three weeks, small sprouts should appear from the eyes. If after four weeks nothing has occurred, the tubers should be exhumed, cooked, and eaten, for they will only have been well stored.

Any potato that has grown successfully in the garden can be overwintered to provide seed stock the following year. The oft-repeated caution that overwintered stock carries diseases that will ruin the crop appears not to be so. In our part of southern Vermont, for example, there are races of potatoes that have been carried from generation to generation for over a hundred years. The old precaution, however, of dusting tubers saved for seed heavily with garden sulfur seems sensible, as a safeguard against overwintering fungus. Tubers reserved for spring planting should be stored at temperatures as close to 40° as can be managed, and by all means kept from frost. Again contrary to frequent advice, potatoes that sprout in storage should not have the pale shoots that may appear broken off. Though many standard potatoes have such vigor that they will indeed sprout and sprout again, the rarer varieties will be too small and fragile to endure such treatment. For years we have planted tubers with thin sprouts sometimes twelve inches long. In such cases, we dig a hole about five inches deep, lift each tuber very carefully from the engangling sprouts of its neighbors, settle it in its hole, and wind its sprouts in a circle about it. The results have always been satisfactory, and the progeny at harvest abundant.

Generally, we plant whole potatoes, though if our stock is short, or if we have ordered in new varieties that are larger than, say, a bantam hen's egg, we will plant "sets," carving up the potato into two or more eyes. Among experienced amateur potato growers, there has always been a dispute about the relative advantages of planting whole tubers versus sets. It does seem true that sets produce larger and more uniform potatoes than do whole tubers, and if that is the home gardener's aim (as it is the aim of large commercial producers), then he should plant sets. Whole tubers, when planted, will produce a much larger number of small potatoes—even marble-size potatoes, and about those we have some thoughts.

"Small potatoes" is generally a term of opprobrium, meaning something worthless, of no account, not to be valued. No common expression could be further from the truth, though we suppose that in times when whole communities depended upon the harvest of potatoes, and only human and animal labor were available, the tedium of gathering in any but the largest tubers must have earned scorn for the small ones. We treasure them all. The large ones, if they do not serve as bakers, are hashed, fried, shredded, mashed, and in many other ways deprived of their integrity. But the small ones are treated with the greatest respect. They are cooked whole, in a variety of ways, never peeled, and they come to the table looking like themselves, but enhanced. When each is an inch long or less and hardly the thickness of a finger, and they are turned constantly in good olive oil heavily scented with garlic until they are crisp on the outside and creamy within, sprinkled toward the end of cooking with fresh rosemary or sage, coarse salt, and pepper, they are like eating vegetable pheasant.

For us, the cultivation of potatoes is, like the cultivation of brassicas (with which they rotate from year to year), simplicity itself. Our light sandy loam is quick to warm in spring, favoring early planting and a long season of growth. We have a high proportion of bright, sunny days in late June and July, when potatoes have their top growth, and summer nights are generally quite cool, perhaps reminding them of their high Andes origins. Rain is abundant and nicely spaced throughout most summers. Were our climate less privileged—for potatoes, at least—we might have many more problems with their culture than we do. So far, we have been mercifully exempt from the worst ills to which potatoes are prone: early blight, late blight, black leg, and verticillium wilt. We do take some precautions, however, by rotating potatoes as best we can with other crops so that they do not grow in the same ground two years running. This means, actually, rotating other members of the *Solanaceae* with them as well, since their cousins in that family—tomatoes, peppers, and eggplants—can exchange the worst diseases among themselves, all of which are soil-borne. Potato beetles were once an annual affliction, and many an early summer morning was devoted to picking off and squashing their destructive little bodies between thumb and forefinger. When they are adults, it is satisfying, actually, in a morbid sort of way, though it is genuinely nasty when they are immature, and simply smear rather than crunch. Now, however, with the bacillus selected specifically for potato beetles (*Bacillus thuringensis* 'San Diego'), that nasty chore is pleasantly in the past.

All our potatoes are planted at more or less the same time in midspring, about two weeks before

❧ *There are many potatoes now on the market with blue skins and flesh. None match more predictably colored varieties for flavor or cooking quality, but for sheer variety they are nice to grow. The variety shown here is the venerable Gurney's 'All Blue,' grown by most vegetable gardeners once at least, as an oddity.*

the last killing frost, which is generally around June 5 here. Were our growing season longer we would make a distinction among varieties, reserving the late-maturing ones for planting two weeks later. But, as with other crops—corn, for example—we have found that our short season causes all our stock to mature at around the same time, no matter how we stagger plantings. It is a good thing, then, that potatoes have the endearing quality of being harvestable at any age. They are not fruits, but rather underground swellings of the root, and one of the great pleasures of high summer is "robbing" the hills. It is stealthy pleasure,

aptly named, and it does seem, to the thrifty gardener capable of delayed gratification, rather a violation of the integrity of the plants. Nevertheless, the urge to rob a hill or two always overtakes us at about the time the peas come in—mid-July for us here—for a few tiny potatoes mixed with them creates one of the treats of the beginning of high summer. To rob a hill, one simply probes gently with one's fingers at the base of a plant until one feels a small, hard knob, which is then gently detached from the roots. It is important not to rob more than one or two potatoes from each hill. If the earth is packed back firmly around the plant and a thorough soaking given, no harm will occur and the plant will go on to produce a respectable crop by autumn digging time.

Potatoes are ready for the main harvest as soon as the flowers fade and the stems begin to yellow. One reads sometimes that potatoes may be left in the ground for two to four weeks after the stems have withered, essentially until the great autumn harvest. We have not found it to be so. Mice are as fond of potatoes as is the gardener, and like many other garden critters, they will spoil more than they eat. They seem to have silver palates, or perhaps they simply weary of eating in the same place night after night. But if one waits too long to harvest, many potatoes in a hill will be nibbled at or even partially consumed. Such potatoes do not store well, for the protective integrity of their skins has been destroyed. They must be discarded into the compost, presumably for the delectation of other mice. It happens often, however, that discarded potatoes or even those missed at harvesttime will endure our harsh winters to sprout in spring, often making quite respectable plants and proving that potatoes are surprisingly hardy.

As recently as ten years ago, unusual potatoes were to be had only in trade with other gardeners, or perhaps from small, obscure catalogs that specialized in heirloom vegetables. Now, however, many catalogs offer them, and interesting forms can even be had, via UPS, from companies that specialize in gourmet foods. Among so many now available, we confess that we have tried only a few, twenty or so—a piddling number, given the possibilities. We mean to keep experimenting, but we doubt that we will ever give up 'Lady Finger.' The name is charming, though we would have to pity the lady with such appendages. 'Lady Finger' is narrow and slightly crescent-shaped, and extremely variable in size, from an

occasional six-inch giant down to tiny tubers half an inch long or less. The skin is a pale, straw yellow, perfect for browning in hot oil, and the flesh is waxy and holds together well when cooked. It is the perfect salad potato, as it retains its character under any amount of dressing. Similar to 'Lady Finger' but somewhat larger and straighter is 'Yellow Banana.' Indeed, the two would be easy to confuse, having the same skin color, the same waxy flesh, and the same uses in the kitchen. 'Yellow Banana' appears to be somewhat more uniform in size and may outdo 'Lady Finger,' already an excellent producer, in abundance.

'Yellow Fir' would be 'Lady Finger' if it could. The flesh is similar, though the skin has an attractive pink blush, as if it had heard something faintly embarrassing just before it was dug. It differs mostly from 'Lady Finger,' however, in the odd knobs and protuberances that form on its crescent-shaped tubers, often giving it a fantastic appearance and making it impossible to peel, should anyone think of doing that sort of thing to it. This potato gives us hope that we will someday unearth a perfect "potato man," and we have come close, though there always seems to be an arm or a leg missing.

'Ruby Crescent' clearly belongs to the clan ruled by 'Lady Finger,' but its name, at least under our growing conditions, creates an annual disappointment. It produces excellent tubers, regular and uniform in size, about three inches long and half an inch thick. At harvesttime, however, we are always sad when we don't pull out of the ground something as richly colored as a jewel or as elegantly shaped as the new moon. To the very imaginative, or in other climates, it might have a faint rosy color. But here it is straw yellow and fairly straight, and assuming we have the true form (always a question, with heirloom potatoes), 'Yellow Kidney' would be a better name. Still, the flavor is good, and the flesh, as with all this group, firm and waxy.

Among true oddities, 'Peruvian Purple' has remained a great favorite of ours. Our first stock was given to us by a Peruvian friend who extracted several tubers from his aunt's refrigerator on a visit to Lima. Later we secured additional stock, carrying the varietal name, 'Peruvian Purple,' though it was virtually identical to the one our friend had brought us, and the two have since been tumbled together in the same seed bin. It produces tubers that are surprisingly uniform in shape and size, scarcely an inch long and wonderfully narrow and straight. The skin is a rich deep purple, tending sometimes almost to mahogany, close to the shade of a fresh ripe prune, but speckled and netted with small brown spots. The flesh is a startling shade of bluish purple, alternating with bands of watery blue if cut lengthwise, and showing an aureole of pale against darker blue if cut crosswise. As there are few edible things in the blue range, 'Peruvian Purple' may be somewhat startling when one first confronts it on the dinner plate. There is also always a faint taste of earth about it, which is pleasing to us, though to others it may be one more reason for passing this cultivar by. All blue potatoes seem to have a relatively high water content and can turn mushy and insipid if overcooked. Therefore, 'Peruvian Purple' is one of the first choices for roasting on the top of the stove in a heavy iron pot in hot, garlic-flavored

❧ *Among all the potatoes one might grow, there should be one at least that is sturdy, sensible, and appropriate to all uses, a sort of backbone potato, suitable for baking, boiling, frying, stewing, and whatever else a potato is good for. Probably the very best potato for any purpose is 'Yukon Gold,' which is rapidly supplanting, in its superb quality, most other standard varieties.*

oil, which somewhat dehydrates it and concentrates its flavor.

There are several other blue potatoes available, among them the one featured first and for many years by Gurney's Seed & Nursery Company. The catalog description is worth quoting in full, because it is vintage Gurney.

Amaze your friends when you ask them over for dinner. Accompany that thick steak with a blue baked potato! Or add color to that roast turkey with bowl of blue mashed potatoes! Or add blue potatoes and orange carrots to a beef roast. Or try ham and scalloped blue potatoes garnished with crumbled blue cheese. This unusual potato is not only blue-skinned but blue-fleshed— through and through! Has good flavor baked or boiled. Makes the potato dish the center of attention. Yields well and is easy to grow. A novelty for the kids to raise. Draws plenty of attention at roadside stands.

'Gurney's Blue,' however remarkable it may be otherwise, is not blue "through and through," at least not in our experience. Rather, it tends to a complex marbling of blue and skim-milk white inside, interesting enough to contemplate, if not to eat. Still, it is certainly a startling potato, and we have carried over stock and grown a few hills for years. The produce is abundant, medium-sized to small, round to oval in shape. Unfortunately, we have found the flesh to be watery and somewhat thin in flavor. Nevertheless, 'Gurney's Blue' is still a fine addition to an Easter-egg arrangement of raw potatoes or to a cooked dish consisting of many colored forms.

Another member of the blue group deserves mention, if only for the fact that it has been treasured for so long in rural Vermont gardens. The origin of 'Cow Horn' is obscure, but its history is rich. Like the Vermont 'Gillifeather' turnip, 'Cow Horn' has been passed on and passed around for over a hundred years. The tubers are hard to keep well anywhere except in the venerable root cellars where they have spent their last century of winters. We have lost seed and begged it again a dozen times. 'Cow Horn' is a large potato, unlike many blues, and with a little imagination it even looks like its name. The skin is a rich bluish purple, and the flesh may be bluish white or quite blue, depending perhaps on the stock one has, or on culture. The texture, surprising in a blue, is mealy and firm. In the garden, as elsewhere, sentiment is a marvelous force in keeping things around. We have not so far found 'Cow Horn' superior to other roasting and baking potatoes, but we keep growing it because our small experience is not prepared to fly in the face of a hundred years of wisdom. "Stands to reason. Folks wouldn't of kept it up if it wasn't good." That is the kind of place we live in, and we accept its values.

Among less eccentric potatoes, 'Urgenta' is very pleasing. We like its name, for one thing, which attests to its early cropping potential, making it a fine candidate for robbing. 'Urgenta' is a medium-sized, reassuringly shaped potato with a waxy yellow skin underlaid with rose. The flesh is waxy also, excellent for roasting, boiling, or salads. Similarly comforting in form is 'Early Rose,' an old standard variety that crops early and should be eaten fresh. We have, however, never gotten any color close to rose from this potato, and we suspect the name may come from a congested formation of eyes at one end of the tuber, which many old reliable varieties show, and which farmers called the "rose end" of the potato. Sets were always carved from this end of the potato, in the conviction that they would produce greater yields than sets carved from other parts. For us, 'Early Rose' is yellowish white, but the flesh is firm and slightly mealy, excellent for all kitchen purposes. It is not, however, a great keeper. With a little experience, one learns to key the consumption of potatoes to the autumn and winter calendar. ("It's almost November. Better finish up the 'Early Rose.') Once deep into potatoes, one thinks this way.

Much more attractively colored is 'Tobique,' a good, standard, all-purpose cultivar whose predominately yellow skin is attractively mottled and blushed with rose. The flesh of 'Tobique' is what might be called "general," neither waxy nor too mealy, but just the sort of texture to stand almost any kitchen treatment. 'Pink Pearl' is much like 'Tobique' in cooking qualities, but a rich orange-pink completely overspreads its skin. On the outside, it is perhaps the prettiest potato we grow. It has also been bred to have eyes that are not recessed, making it a good candidate for those who insist on peeling a potato. But its best use is perhaps for boiling, as red "new" potatoes, for its skin retains much of its color under cooking, and is attractive sprinkled with fresh parsley.

'Brigus' is a fine, bold-looking potato (as its name seems to imply), with a skin of a color hard to pin down. Patches somewhere between ox-blood and mahogany appear to break through its russet netting. The skin is quite thick, made for potato-skin connoisseurs. The flesh is mealy, suiting it for baking when smeared with a coat of olive oil and with a clean nail driven into its heart for even, rapid cooking. No matter how well washed, it still possesses the faint earth taste that seems typical of many dark-skinned potatoes.

Various bright yellow–fleshed potatoes have come into our garden under different names—'Yellow Rose,' 'Yellow Apple,' 'Finnish Yellow,' and originally, from a gourmet food market, "the butterless potato," which is almost certainly the celebrated 'Yukon Gold.' All of them seem to have the sweetest of all potato flesh, as sweet as many apples, and in fact too sweet for some true potato lovers. They are all neat and round, fairly small in size, born to be the delight of dieters. The flesh of all is a uniform yellow, causing them to look as if they have been buttered even when they have not. Sublime as hash browns, they also make superior potato salad, especially when (and contrary to received culinary wisdom) they are not boiled whole and then cubed, but rather, cubed raw and simmered in salted boiling water until just tender.

We begin our consumption of potatoes in high summer, with the precious few we are bold enough to rob from the growing hills. By early autumn, when most have been dug, they become almost a staple of our evening meal, absent only when pastas are cooked, or when some dish seems to demand rice. Stored in the shed of the lower greenhouse and carefully protected from light (which turns them green and poisonous) they last through late autumn and winter, until the advent of dandelion season, when we crave lighter, more tonic things. Thereafter, when a potato is needed, it is apt to come from the supermarket. Such potatoes are, of course, only a faint memory of the good ones we have grown and eaten throughout the darker months, and according to our deepest beliefs about cooking and eating, they are little more than study indefensibles, reflecting the common belief that a potato is just, after all, a potato. Nothing, of course, could be further from the truth.

Beyond potatoes and the large and varied world of brassicas, two other crops become prominent in late autumn, the one common enough, and the other rather rare. The common one is leeks, though familiar as they are, they are a much neglected vegetable in American kitchens. They are delightfully easy to raise. From an early-spring sowing under glass of fat black seed, they can be transplanted as mere green hairs into the garden as soon as the soil can be worked and they are big enough. Spacing is always a big issue for the greedy home gardener, and too many crops are sown or planted far too thickly—potatoes, for example, or radishes or heading lettuces. But leeks may be transplanted into rows with hardly four inches between one seedling and another, and still they will make thick white columns of growth, their handsome gray-green flags of leaf fanned one against the other. That is not the way, of course, to grow prize-winning leeks, with huge, arm-thick trunks. But one huge leek is no better in the kitchen than two or three smaller ones (and no worse either); but when one needs only a little leek, for a soup, perhaps, half a big one will go to waste. Smaller leeks, besides, can be cooked whole, browned in butter and braised in chicken stock and then—if the meal is meager otherwise or one feels fancy—dusted with gratings of hard cheese and bread crumbs and browned for a wonderful gratin. Two or three small leeks will serve one person, but it is hard to split up a big leek at the table, and the results always look a little messy and chewed on.

Besides their economical use of space, leeks are very easy to grow in the home garden. They ask (as do almost all other vegetables) a deep, humus-rich soil and plenty of moisture during their long growing season. A little granular fertilizer, such as 5-10-10, is very beneficial, applied once, a week or two after they have caught hold as transplants, and then a month later. Otherwise, they ask only to be kept weeded, though one must never cultivate deeply around their roots, which are shallow and easily damaged. Best of all, perhaps, leeks are one of

several crops that do not require the very best light. A tomato will be a very poor thing in half a day of shade, but lettuce, celery, celeriac, radishes, and leeks will be at least decent. They can be made to produce the longest white stalks by blanching them in a number of cunning ways, most artfully perhaps by setting a terra cotta drain tile over each plant, with only its head of leaves sticking out. A wonderful effect can be contrived that way, and for really creative gardeners, an enfilade of leeks in tiles could make a splendid edging to a central garden path. But one need not bother otherwise. For from a twelve-foot row of free-growing leeks, or the edging to a six-foot square bed within which other crops are grown, plenty of leeks will be harvested for most kitchens.

Leeks are among the hardiest of all vegetable plants, so much so that even when their columns of stem are filled with ice, they may be dug and stored for winter. Indeed, where garden temperatures do not fall much below 15° they may be left in the ground, harvested all winter and into spring, or allowed, in their second season, to produce three-foot-tall stems topped with a globe of dusty purple allium flowers the size of a large orange. Storage is very simple. Plants are dug or even simply pulled from the ground, their roots trimmed away, and as much of their tops cut off as one wishes to sacrifice. (For, though only the white part of the leek is generally treasured in most kitchens, the greens are valuable additions to soups, stir-fries, or even rice.) The great trick in preparing leeks for storage is not to cut away the basal plate, a disclike area of firm flesh at the end of the stalk, for it holds the leek together and encourages it to think, in winter storage, that it might live another life, come spring. The leeks are then bundled into plastic bags and stored in the refrigerator, or, if space is lacking there, in a

Leeks are even easier to grow than other members of the onion clan, and being frost-hardy, may be allowed to stand after most other garden crops are harvested, even until collars of ice form about their stems. They will be the sweeter in flavor for that, and will keep better as well, either because they have already approached refrigerator temperatures in the open, or because, harvested late, they will spend less time in its clammy gloom.

Puntarelle is a handsome, thin-bladed chickory, grown not for its leaves, which are very bitter, but for its crunchy leaf stalks. They will be bitter, too, unless they have endured some cold. Further, they must be split with a thin knife into halves or quarters and plunged into ice water. Under this treatment, they become milder in flavor and curl engagingly into corkscrew shapes. They are always served alone, as a salad, with a special dressing rich in garlic and anchovies.

quite cold, dark spot where temperatures hover just above freezing. After a winter chill, they become quite mild, and the tender inner parts can be shredded lengthwise, soaked in ice water until they curl, and dressed with olive oil and balsamic vinegar for a pleasant winter salad.

Even better for that purpose is puntarelle, a member of the chicory family that has been grown around Rome for late-autumn and winter salads for centuries, and indeed is so naturalized that it can be gathered from roadside ditches. It is a beautiful plant, not open-headed or cabbage-y as are many other garden chicories, but tall and straight, with lance-shaped, dark green–bladed leaves atop two-foot stems. It is the stems that

one eats, though preparing them is a deal of labor, hardly justifiable except that they are so good, and fresh salads are mostly scarce in late autumn. Puntarelle is sown directly into rows in spring, rather closely spaced, and the plants must be encouraged to grow free and strong all summer. They are not good for much, however, until really cool weather, and even frost. Puntarelle is practically the last green thing we take from the garden. It can be harvested for about a month and a half, from mid-September until the end of October, though at the end of that period lengths of burlap should be thrown across the rows to protect the plants from really severe frosts. Whole bunches are severed at ground level

❧ *Figs are hardly a crop to be grown in the open ground of southern Vermont, but so fond are we of fresh figs that we keep three trees in large terra-cotta pots. They are very decorative grown that way, but with luck, they will also produce figs by autumn—though never enough. This one is the ancient variety 'Panache,' with fruits striped green and yellow.*

and brought to the kitchen, where the dark leaves are trimmed away, leaving only the pale, lettuce-green stems. Each stem is then split with the tip of a sharp knife, either in half or in quarters, depending on its width. The stems are plunged into quite cold water, and left there until they curl into spirals and some of their bitterness is drawn off. Then they are spun or patted dry, and coated with a quite rich dressing of strongly flavored good olive oil, minced garlic, vinegar, and two or three anchovy fillets mashed to a paste. The result is far from a spring or summer salad, where everything is light and delicate. Rather, it is an autumn salad, firm and crunchy and almost celerylike, appropriate to the richer meals of late autumn.

Puntarelle essentially closes down our long season of eating fresh things directly from the garden. There may be a late sowing of spinach worth harvesting, a few late beets or turnips, a row of mesclun—even, with luck, a handful of radishes. Certainly there will be kale, if we feel like taking it. But from now until spring, we must depend largely on our store of cabbages and Brussels sprouts, of potatoes, carrots, beets, 'Black Spanish' radishes, and turnips. It is their season now, and we will relish them, preparing them with care and taking care to return to them—through slow cooking, lacings of wine or cream, cheese or herbs—something of, even something more than, all they offered us, fresh from the garden. It is always good to have a rest from any labor, even from any pleasure, for then one comes back to it more eagerly. Soon the catalogs will arrive, and we will begin the planning of next year's vegetable garden, adding new varieties, seeking out those we have had before. Meanwhile, and for the next three months, the garden sleeps, and the part of it that is us sleeps too. We've all worked hard, and are not sorry for the rest.

Winter

Suddenly it is late November. An icy rain began falling deep in the night, somewhere around three, and, as with any nighttime change in the weather, at any season, we woke briefly, or half woke, to register the change. Toward dawn rain turned to snow. Accumulations of a foot or more are predicted throughout the day, schools are closed, and the nearest airports, Hartford and Albany, are iced in, passengers stranded. There is no traffic on the road. The first major storm has caught everyone by surprise, but the small birds that gathered yesterday in the garden, greedily stocking up on frost-soft crab apples and the berries of the deciduous hollies we had not netted, must have known and taken flight in the dusk. Their chatter is now absent, as is all sound but the quiet shush of snow falling, fast now by noon, and promised to continue throughout the day to midnight. With one definitive stroke, autumn has now ended, and winter has begun.

Winter—such as it can be, here in southern Vermont—requires a lot, first to learn and then to love. Other seasons ask their due, largely of relentless labor and an exacting obedience to the schedules they impose. But winter is at once easier and more difficult than any of them. Its difficulties are those of darkness, of cold, and of length. Winter in Vermont can seem much longer than any other season, robbing unfairly from both the autumn and the spring to augment its time. At its deepest cold, winter here can threaten all life, and one knows in one's very bones that life is made possible only by forethought and provision. Many of our provisions have been at best halfhearted. Our clothes are not warm enough, reflecting neither adequate bulk, which we hate as an encumbrance to our movements, nor the latest slick technology in man-made fibers. Our house, with its oversized paned glass windows and its glassed-in winter garden just off the kitchen, would make any specialist in heat efficiency throw up his hands in despair. Some sections of the house are at best drafty, and really cold weather can be judged by the fact that the bolts on our heavy wooden doors are frosted on the inside, and a dusting of snow builds up on the jamb within. Our storm sashes, which we insist be of wood and glass, never get put up on time; and even when they are finally in place and padded with felt strips at their edges, they are still apt to show a haze of fog at each side and even, in coldest weather, a skin of clear ice.

Fortunately, our provisions against darkness have been more spirited, as befits defense against an enemy that strikes the mind and heart, and not the body. Ours is a house of many fireplaces, one in each major room, and they burn each day, all day, from late autumn until spring. We know that they are not an efficient way to augment the heat of a house, since even with the best fire-place, 90 percent or more of the heat escapes up the draft of the flue. But we depend on their light and life far more than on their warmth. Rekindling them at morning provides a beginning to the day, and adding a log or two offers a break from mental work and its fatigues as the day progresses. At evening, when dark comes, they burn their brightest, and then, at bedtime, they are banked for the long night ahead, the day closing with a task that fitly concludes the way it began. Our fires of course require labor to maintain, but it is lucky that we live deep in the woods, and can feed them (and thus our spiritual selves) through the cutting and splitting of logs, the hauling and stacking of wood in the barn, the replenishing of piles next to each fireplace, upstairs and down. We are grateful for the physical work in a season so lacking in other forms of meaningful physical exercise. And as long as we can manage five heavy split logs apiece (which is longer by far, we imagine, than we could without their burden), we will be grateful for the labor.

We have found another stratagem—perhaps a subterfuge—for extending our winter light. We keep our own time. Some years ago, when we gave up teaching and the alarm clock, both together, through inattention we failed to set back our clocks in October to standard time. It did not take long for us to discover our error, but we found that the extra hour of light at the end of the day was far more precious to us than an hour's early start in the morning. As we no longer needed to go out into the world at all, or at least not according to the world's schedule, we elected to stay on daylight saving time permanently. So what the world in the morning calls six we call seven, finding it pleasant to wake later with the light. At four or four-thirty, when darkness falls for the rest of the world, here at North Hill it is still twilight, a nice time to begin thinking of preparing supper.

By these maneuvers, we have come to tolerate winter, and even to love it. We could perhaps love it even better still if we could work in our garden, garnering its fresh produce for each day's meal at the end of each day's labor. When fits of winter impatience have come on us (as they will, no matter what), we have sometimes entertained the fantasy that we could escape winter altogether, abandon the cows and poultry, the tender greenhouse plants, drain our pipes and let our fireplaces go cold, lock our doors and turn our backs on cold and dark. We could live, for the winter at least, in another place entirely, one full of light and warmth and—the main thing for us—gardening. But putting aside financial considerations (which are large) and our love for our animals (some of whom are quite large, too, hardly acceptable by any airline in "pet carriers"), we know that we are firmly rooted in place, in a single place, This Place, and that a bifurcated existence would suit us hardly better than the dreadful mental disorder of schizophrenia. So we manage, even in the darkest days, to eat from our garden. Now, though, we harvest from the root cellar rather than from the earth.

Oh, of course we do cheat. Lettuces, for example, do not store, though we have flirted with trying to make them do it, by lifting autumn-tight heads of 'Reine des Glaces' or 'Merveille de Quatres Saisons,' both names so promising of this possibility. Packed in boxes, essentially transplanted with lots of earth about their roots and kept in good light, they are useful for two or three weeks past their proper time of survival in the garden. A hunger, too, for some of the more fragile brassicas—broccoli, cauliflower, or bitter broccoli rabe—*will* come on us by late December or early January, and that must be satisfied. But we always wonder, when we have given in, whether the consequences were worth

the compromise we made with principle. Principle, of course, is to eat what we have actually raised, to ingest into our bodies only what we directly know went into the crop, and only what we know will still be good, and good for us, even if that crop is harvested two or three months before its consumption. The blandishments of the supermarket (though we confess they are sometimes irresistible) are rather like pornography. That is, the urges exist more in imagination than in reality: and that bunch of asparagus spears—so perfectly aligned, so green and dewy fresh—is apt to promise more than it can give. Real loves are always best. For though they may fall short of visual perfection and be a little worn and stale in their dress, there is still depth in them. In winter, we depend on those things that can be counted on to last, not losing much of their essential quality in the process.

Throughout the late autumn, crops have been taken up and put in storage to produce a winter's worth of meals. Now, a new ritual orders the end of the day. It is the walk to the lower greenhouse, which lies perhaps five or six hundred feet from the kitchen door, down through the garden to its lowest end. At last light of day (in January, about four-thirty here, but three-thirty by the world's time) it can sometimes be a wholly pleasant trek. Snow may be thin enough only to mark one's path down and back, or deep enough to make one a sort of human snowplow, requiring one to save breath, while carrying a burden of produce, by carefully fitting step to step uphill, along the path one made coming down. In the first case, our big collie will dash madly from side to side, hoping for a squirrel to chase across the crust of snow, and a troupe of three or four of the house cats may come along, just for the pleasure of taking the air in good company. But in the second, the dog will tread patiently behind, in the path

Even at the beginning of winter, the vegetable garden, stripped of its crops and composted, has a certain somber beauty. Here in November, at least the idea of something to gather made it a good idea to carry up a harvesting bucket, for there are always a few late lettuces, a row of mesclun, or a few stems of puntarelle for an early-winter salad.

we have made, and all the cats will remain in their warm nests of barn straw, wondering at the lunacy that would make anyone choose to sink hip-deep in cold snow. But either way, the journey is a good time to look at the garden, to admire the gaunt outlines of deciduous trees and shrubs, the fine dark architecture of the conifers, to study the trails of the many small creatures we never actually see, and to determine—by sharp tracks, piles of droppings, or the telltale sign of a nibbled branch—whether deer have broken through our defense of walls and tall electric fences. For once they have found their way in, they will return, nibbling our world to nothing. In such a case, no matter how tired we are or how deep the snow, immediate intervention is required.

Those are the pleasant trips; there is a third type, frequent enough in its occurrence, that requires pure discipline. It is when bitter winds are blowing, the temperature is at minus something dreadful, and swirls of icy snow seem not so much a phenomenon of nature as a malevolent force, bent, with pure sentient malice, on exterminating us in our tracks. On such evenings we would probably choose to go hungry, or to depend on whatever has already been brought up to the house, rather than make the trip down. But we do not actually have the choice, because on such days the greenhouse seems a pathetically fragile structure. It is heated by propane gas, the reservoirs of which we take great care to keep well stocked, and it is very well insulated. Nevertheless, mechanical failures can occur (and have), necessitating firing up auxiliary kerosene heaters, and a long night of vigilance until repairs can be made.

Fortunately, such dire occurrences have been rare. And in any weather, the evening trip down to the greenhouse has its reward, or rather, two

rewards. The first is that once one has gotten there, shoveled away the snow from the wooden storm door (which opens outward), and forced free the frozen bolt of the glass door (which opens inward), one enters an enchanted world, full of warmth and fragrance and the quiet smell of the living earth. *Buddleia asiatica* will be blooming, and *Osmanthus fragrans* will almost overpower us with its honey scent produced from tiny white flowers, surely the sweetest in the plant kingdom for the flower's size. There will be geraniums, scarlet and salmon against the icy windows, and rosemaries—the old standard-trained trees that ornament the vegetable garden in summer and are stored here in large pots for the winter—to touch or to harvest. It will be the season, too, for tiny species cyclamen—*Cyclamen cicilium* and *C. cicilium* 'Album,' *C. africanum, C. graecum,* and the more familiar *C. hederifolium* and *coum*—none of which are hardy for us outdoors, but all so easy to manage in pots, sleeping out the summer and coming to life when we need them most, in the depths of winter.

The second reward lies beyond, in the darkened chamber, where we have stored provisions for the winter's table. There are the stone crocks of beets, carrots, turnips, and 'Black Spanish' radishes packed in moist sand. There are wooden wine crates of potatoes, sorted by variety, more than we can eat in a winter, and thus enough for planting stock come spring. Cabbages lie heaped in one cold corner, covered with burlap, their outer leaves more rotted and odiferous as winter

❦ RIGHT: *The goodness of roots sustains us, like lesser creatures, throughout the winter. Beets, here the variety 'Chiogga,' banded inside with red and gold, rest among withered leaves until they may be carried to the storage shed, where their leaves will be cut away and the roots buried in damp cold sand until they are needed.*

LEFT: *The apple season extends in southern Vermont from August well into November, each antique variety ripening in succession for a continuous supply of fruit. It is the last to ripen that keep best, however, and the very best of them is the old English variety, 'Cox's Orange Pippin.' Not orange at all, but a fiery scarlet red, it should be gathered even after frost has withered its leaves.*

progresses, but their hearts firm and solid. The Brussels sprouts too are there, whole stalks stood upright with the garden dirt still about their roots, a crop to harvest until sometime past the New Year. On rustic wooden tables is our store of apples, chiefly the fine old variety called 'Cox's Orange Pippin,' in our opinion the very best of the old sort, a late ripener and an excellent keeper. Just lately pears have joined them, though it will be a few years yet before our own young pear trees produce anything like the crops we regularly harvest from the twenty-year-old antique apple trees that form the back boundary of the perennial garden.

Perhaps the most precious of all the things stored in the shed is our hoard of endives. Actually, they are not so much stored as growing, in a sense, for forced endive is the only salad crop we have found we can culture with ease in winter. Much like the vast array of brassicas, all chicories grown in gardens for their leaves are descendents of one wild progenitor, *Cichorium intybus* var. *foliosum*, which has over the centuries been bred for distinct leaf characteristics, flavors, and kitchen uses. Within the clan are some of the choicest of all salad greens, such as the Venetian chicories known as radicchio, the red chicory

We do only as much chemical spraying as is absolutely necessary, so few of the apples we produce will be without some blemish or scar. Still, they are beautiful, as are beautiful faces that have never known any surgical intervention.

❧ *The very last crop of all to be harvested from the garden is chicory, best taken after frost has blackened the leaves. After it is dug up, the gate of the garden will be tied shut, and there will be no further reason to enter it until it is time for the first spring sowings.*

called 'Rossa di Treviso' and the beautiful red and green streaked 'Rossa di Verona,' which, for all their current fashionableness as "gourmet" vegetables, are heirlooms from the eighteenth century. Within the group is also succory, the wild chicory (actually a Colonial garden escapee) that flourishes along roadsides, ornamenting them in summer with its limpid-blue flowers. But for us, the greatest treasure in the group is winter chicory, or Belgian endive, grown not as a summer salad crop (for its summer leaves are *very* bitter; we have tried them) but for its roots, which may be forced into growth in winter.

Not guessing how easy it is to force Belgium endive, we maintained a sneaking supermarket addiction to it, for actually, as our relish is for its crunchy texture and its only slightly bitter flavor,

it is among the most reliable of all supermarket "crops." Then one year we decided to try forcing our own, and we have never looked back since. Belgium endive must be sown in spring, at the same time as first lettuces and other salad crops, but it is left to grow in rows throughout the summer season and well into autumn. It asks only to be kept free of weeds (though it is competitive, even there) and fertilized occasionally with granular 5-10-10 to produce the largest possible roots. As late in the autumn as we dare to wait (which is just before hard frost makes digging impossible), the plants are lifted and the top growth cut back to within an inch or so of the root top. The white, carrotlike roots are then placed in large containers with their tops six to eight inches below the rim. For economy of

❧ *Chickory roots are trimmed of their tops and made ready for insertion into barely damp peat. One huge pot, used in summer to grow annuals, will accommodate our entire crop and provide two months of harvest in the depths of winter.*

space, the roots may almost touch. Though almost any old container will do—even white plastic buckets or oversized black plastic nursery cans—we use the huge old terra-cotta pots that in summer ornament the garden here and there, planted to annuals, figuring that as they must be put under cover for the winter anyway, they might as well be put to this pleasant use.

In the beginning we packed the endive roots in sand, as we would any other root crop for winter storage. That was a huge mistake, for cut them apart and wash them how we would, we could never quite free the witloofs from a bite of grit in the teeth, in no way pleasant in any salad. So now we use pure peat (obviously, organic and sterile) in the pleasant expectation that if a shred or two of it gets through the wash, it will only look like a fleck of pepper, and not cost a bit of enamel from a tooth. When the first snouts of growth appear at the surface of the peat, we feel down gently for the roots to which they are attached, pull them out (easy, if the medium is barely moistened peat), and sever each just where growth and root crown meet. Usually, the first harvest will be of perfectly formed, oval witloofs, very close in perfection to those displayed in the supermarket, and far superior in flavor. But the thrifty reinsertion of roots from which the first harvest has been taken will produce another growth, not oval but bunched, rather like small lettuces. Those may be left to extend above the surface of the peat and take on a pale-green color. After all harvests are complete, the roots may be exhumed from the peat in early spring and planted in a meadow garden or along the roadside, eventually to blend their flowers, mauve or paler blue, with the clear-blue ones of succory.

Though we try to keep our winter storage shed as full of produce as possible, certain things are kept in the cellar of the house, either because they last better there or because they are just the things we might relish for a quick nibble between meals or to improve a stock or soup. Chiefly these are celeriac and leeks, put in plastic bags (we could of course use oiled parchment, but we are not so pure as that) and kept in an old refrigerator bought twenty years ago for fifteen dollars. There, both keep in good condition throughout the winter, and as gaps open among the piles of them, paper-white narcissus in pots take up the space. For, though good results can be had with paper-whites when grown on straight after potting, better results occur if they are allowed to root in a cool, dark place, as one would do with any other forced bulb. In the basement also are winter squash and pumpkins, those that have not been arranged for decoration under the hall table, for we grow too many to fit there—too many generally, perhaps, though they make easily portable winter feasts for the poultry. On shelves are jars of oil-baked tomatoes, the base of many a winter's pasta, and apple sauce and preserves: currant, gooseberry, strawberry, and raspberry, all from our own plants. The pickles there are only of one sort, the precious supply of bread-and-butter pickles our neighbor and friend, Faith Sprague, still supplies us with, though she is now well past ninety, and so has warned us to be frugal with them.

Sharing the basement is the freezer, though no produce from the garden rests in it. Rather, it is full of beef and veal and chicken, pork or lamb (and once, goat), all raised here in conditions we believe are humane and pleasant. We have already written of the effort the raising of veal requires: constant bottle-feeding of rich, creamy milk over the calf's whole life. The beef we raise is easier, for the cows are on pasture, and are penned and fed grain for only a few weeks at the end, to induce the fatty marbling that so much improves the savor of the meat. We know, of course, that lean beef would be much more healthful. But we do not care, for the main purpose of life is not the avoidance of a heart attack. We live lives here that are full of exercise and healthy labor, and we ingest perhaps more than our share of broccoli and savory tomatoes, of garlic, olive oil, and red wine, all conducive to longevity. But to all those we add some pleasures that are less healthful, too: some red meat and rich cheese and even an occasional smoke.

But even with the graining, our beef is still leaner than commercially available beef. The breed we keep, Scots Highlands, is lean by nature. They graze and browse all their lives, grain being offered only at the end. They therefore also never know the horrors of a feedlot, heavy doses of hormones and antibiotics laced into their rations, or the chaotic slaughter of their kind around them. And even when one is slaughtered, the meat is aged naturally, not chemically, as is most commercial beef. It is allowed to hang a month or more to reach, on the outside at least, the very cusp of decay that produces the tenderest and most flavorful beef. Those used to the rather bland taste of supermarket beef might find it startling, and we have been told that its flavor is much closer to that of game—venison or elk—than of beef. That, of course, seems an advantage to us, and the beef we raise, though it may not produce a steak identical to what might be had in the poshest American steakhouse, stands up magnificently to the long, slow stewing we usually tend, in any case, to find more interesting.

In the odd year we raise a lamb as well. Bought in April from a local fold, the lamb is led out each morning to feast on grass in the meadow and even the lawns of the garden. That requires careful adjustment of its tether, because it would, of course, be just as happy—happier, perhaps—with mouthfuls of daylily or dianthus than grass. But greater disasters than that can occur. Once, while we were working at the other end of the property, our summer lamb was attacked by a pack of dogs and injured so badly that we had no choice but to put it down and bury it. To ensure against such a catastrophe ever occurring again, the next dog we acquired (for here, there must be a dog) was a rough-coat collie. The breed is sweet and gentle with all our domestic animals, the cats (who are quite fond of him as well), the chickens, and the geese, though he cannot be broken of the satisfying conviction that they are to be herded into neat little groups. A visiting child is, for him, pure bliss. He is, however, fierce in his need to protect and secure his property and all the creatures meant to live here against dogs and coyotes and fisher cats, and anything else that would do harm to what he considers his responsibility to protect. To our delight as gardeners, he also considers rabbits, squirrels, groundhogs, and raccoons fair game, though he only chases them madly back behind the electric cow fence and into the woods, and has never succeeded in catching one, if indeed that is his intent. He has been trained as well never to walk or run through a flower bed or ornamental planting, and that has not actually been a difficult thing to do, requiring only patience and firmness, for part of the richness of his lineage is a respect for boundaries.

Lovers of animals that we are, we have nevertheless come to the conviction that blood matters in any domestic animal, and certainly in one who is expected not only to be an amiable pet but also to do his share of work around the place. Mutts of indeterminate breed from the local animal shelter may be charming, but one never knows for sure what compulsions may lie deep in their nature, ready to surface, to the enormous frustration of their owners. Even dogs of certified lineage should be chosen for the specific capacities bred into them over many generations. Our first dog here was a magnificent Irish setter, fabulously intelligent and deeply affectionate. But being a field dog, her nature was to roam, and her need for athletic activity was as fierce as that of any Olympic competitor. When she hit her stride, twenty miles or more was nothing to her. We know that, because we would often whistle ourselves hoarse with anxiety at her absence, and then wait for the telephone call, which invariably informed us that our dog was visiting in a neighboring town. She was willful, too, and somewhat stubborn, absolutely respecting our requirement that she keep out of the garden beds when she was under our eye, but leaving telltale signs that she had prowled them at will when we were away, or sleeping. Nor did she have any great sense of responsibility for other animals on the place. Once she understood that they were not legitimate field game, they simply bored her. So our next choice, and our subsequent one, has been for rough-coat collies, different from show collies—the Lassie type—in that all their protective instincts, bred into them for many generations, have not been sacrificed for increased beauty. They are beautiful enough, as a breed, being stocky and solid and thick of coat and completely winter-hardy for the occasional night duty in winter that they must perform. We have had two, and will have a third, when we must, without asking any further questions.

If, in a given year, we have not raised a lamb, then we are likely to have raised a pig. More to the point, at the moment we are raising a pig. Lambs and calves are always summer-raised and slaughtered before the onset of cold weather.

Properly, pigs should be so as well, to take advantage of the surplus of the garden, split cabbages, woody radishes, bean and pea vines with overripe pods on them, bolted lettuces, and the like—for, unlike other domestic animals (chickens excepted), the diet of a pig is as broad as the diet of humans, and a pig will eat anything we eat, compromising not in variety, but only in gourmet standards. Nevertheless, when we raise a pig, we always do it in winter. Farmers would consider that a perversion, but, to be frank, as clean as we keep his stall (and that is very clean indeed) he will be smelly. (That is, to be franker still, another of the many resemblances between pigs and people.) We ourselves do not object even to that, for country smells go with country living, and liking the latter so much, we have had perforce to become inured to the former. In any case, there is nothing so beneficial to a garden as pig manure, and as gardeners, we count that all as thrift. The fact is that in summer, we have many visitors who, while delighting in the beauty of the garden (and little guessing at the substances on which it actually depends), might object to the conjunction of summer odors—lilac and rose, lily and . . . pig. One in particular, our friend Martha Ronk, migrates here each summer to spend a month in her own cabin in the woods. She is very sensitive of nose, to the point that we had once very bluntly to say to her, "Very well, Martha, go *bathe* the cows!" We know that a pig would push her hard.

That is not the only problem with keeping a pig. Of all domestic animals raised for food, none are more personable, more charming, or more intelligent than pigs. Successful movies have been made of the fact. It does require a certain dissociation of sensibility and natural affection to come to know, rather well, actually, someone you intend to eat. There is nothing much to a calf, or even a cow. We endow them with personalities, out of our need to see reflections of ourselves in the natural world. But really, both are only a mouth, perhaps a limpid and beautiful set of eyes, and the most stubborn sense of order and routine in the whole panoply of domestic animals. ("Nothing," Thoreau says, "regulates like a cow.") But pigs require no transfer of characteristics from the human personality to be found amiable. They are cute, and smart, and, actually, terribly concerned with their personal cleanliness. They will order the little worlds of their stalls like one-room efficiency apartments, selecting one warm corner for a bed (which they fluff and make up each morning), and another for a toilet. As long as the stall is kept clean and fresh, they will never confuse either arrangement with their dining room, where food is served. If they roll in mud (or, lacking mud, in other things) that is only because their skins tend to be very dry, without sweat glands, and who is actually to say that they would not prefer a nice rub with Eucerin or Nivea? Certainly they like a good scratch behind the ears, and a really thorough backrub.

It is perhaps a good thing, then, that pigs have in them another element of the human personality. They are very stubborn. As they reach puberty, they become more stubborn, and when they arrive at approximately two hundred pounds of young adulthood, they are more stubborn still. It has been true of every pig we have raised that when its end drew near, we heaved an enormous sigh of relief. That is not at all because of the exacting routine of feeding, about which we (and the pig) are very particular. It is true, of course, that a pig eats a surprising amount of food, and we are unwilling to depend on the commercially available bagged products, with strange and uncertain ingredients in them. So we boil up larger and larger amounts of cracked corn and molasses, rice and vegetables, Cream of Wheat (of which pigs are particularly fond), or savory stews made of all the oddments left over in the refrigerator. We are even glad for this labor, which cleans the cupboards and the refrigerator of things we would no longer wish to eat, making of them, for the time the pig is with us, something other than food museums. But all of that is simply the responsibility of tending a life one has chosen to bring into one's world, and the labor is not resented. The reason for the sigh of relief is that we get tired of being bossed and bullied and sometimes bitten, and very often grumbled at. So in the end, something occurs that is rather like a divorce. But of course, we eat the pig.

The labors of winter are steady and predictable, and they tend to open and close each day. First, the cows must be fed, two bales up to their feeding place each morning, and two bales at twilight. In winter they do not venture far. Then, two five-gallon plastic buckets must be filled with water at the house and taken up to the chickens and geese. They must be released from their coops, to come out and bask in the wan winter sun, if there is any. The geese will always risk the trip out of their house, in any weather, for they are wonderfully well insulated against the cold, and they are intelligent and curious, needing to see each day whether the world looks as it did the day before. In that they are just like folks. But at twilight they will be obedient, waddling like ships through the snow to their warm shelter, glad, we think, for the care we take to secure them from a bitter night. The pigeons in the barn loft will need fresh water brought to them too, so that they do not have to fly far to search for it and can huddle against the house chimney, made comfortingly warm by the fires within. Porridge must be boiled up for the pig,

Though tough and sturdy, all our poultry are just as glad not to venture from their warm house on a cold, early-winter day. Their bodies, sometimes quite tiny, are little furnaces that heat the building during the day, helped by the wan winter light, and keep it warmer at night.

and cooled a bit, though he relishes it quite warm. The cats must be fed, our five handsome Maine coons, gloriously thick-coated with winter fur and content, by heritage, with winter itself. But they cannot be fed, for all their insistence, until all other chores are completed, for we like their company as we go about our work, and anyway, while we went about our rounds our collie would eat up all we put in their bowls. In any weather the greenhouse must be checked to see that it is snug and warm and that its tender and tropical plants have not dried out. Morning and evening, armloads of firewood must be brought in from the barn, and in between, we work at other things, or rest. In the twilight we check the greenhouse for the final time, and gather our supper, or at least whatever component of it is something we grew.

Those are the tasks of winter, and they are pleasurable, once one submits to their rhythm, their inexorable necessity. There is pleasure, too, in moving about the garden at this season. Familiar plants are transformed by their burdens of snow and ice, voids and vistas appear that we know in summer are full. The way the wind sculpts the snow is endlessly delightful, if one is not hostile to the medium itself or blinded by the cold. Oddly, most oddly, there are sections of the winter garden that are fragrant, faintly but perceptibly, from sources (perhaps frozen bark or sap, perhaps certain rotted leaves) that we have never identified. On the coldest, coldest days, there is still also life, or the evidence of it. Tracks are everywhere, identifiable by their shape and distance one from the other, and we have seen tiny spiders creeping across the snow, even in temperatures almost life-threatening to us. A flock of wild turkeys may be ahead in our path, as tame almost as domestic fowl, but wary, moving off into the shelter of the woods. A jay, improbably blue in a white world, will flash through the trees, and the inky elegance of a crow might, for a moment, give depth to the gray of the woods. The year is almost over. And that is to say, for as long as we can do what we are doing here, that it is about to begin.

Even in the snow of December, a few persistent Brussels sprouts endure. They might be worth gathering, to bake in parchment envelopes with marble-sized potatoes, small carrots, a clove of garlic, and a sprig of rosemary. Or, stiff with ice as they are, they might be brought to the poultry house, whose inhabitants would find them a delightful and unexpected surprise.

INDEX

Index